MASS
ON
SUNDAY

MASS ON SUNDAY

AND OTHER WAYS OF BEING CATHOLIC

Charles E. Miller, C.M.

Paulist Press
New York/Mahwah, N.J.

Imprimi potest:
Bernard J. Quinn, C.M.
Provincial, Vincentian Province of the West

Nihil obstat:
Richard Albarano
Censor Deputatus

Imprimatur:
Cardinal Roger Mahony
Archbishop of Los Angeles
May 1, 2002
Memorial of St. Joseph the Worker

Aside from the opening epigraph, which is the author's own translation, scripture extracts are taken from the New Revised Standard Version, Copyright © 1989, by the Division of Christian Education of the National Council of the Churches of Christ in the United States of America and reprinted by permission of the publisher.

Cover design by Sharyn Banks
Book design by Lynn Else

Library of Congress Cataloging-in-Publication Data

Miller, Charles Edward, 1929–
   Mass on Sunday : and other ways of being Catholic / Charles E. Miller.
     p. cm.
   ISBN 0-8091-4237-6 (alk. paper)
   1. Christian life—Catholic authors. 2. Catholic Church—Doctrines. 3. Catholic Church—Liturgy. I. Title.

   BX2350.3.M55 2004
   282—dc22
                                                           2004002204

Published by Paulist Press
997 Macarthur Boulevard
Mahwah, New Jersey 07430

www.paulistpress.com

Printed and bound in the United States of America

CONTENTS

By your gift I will proclaim your praise in the vast assembly.
(Ps 22:26)

PREFACE
My Plan for This Book

The aim of such instruction is love that comes from a pure heart, a good conscience, and sincere faith. (1 Tim 1:5)

The first thing I wanted to do in writing this book was to emphasize the celebration of Mass on Sunday as essential to being a Catholic. That had to be the initial chapter. From it flowed an account of my own personal reason for being a Catholic. I thought that emphasis on the Mass led to a brief treatment of adoration of the Blessed Sacrament. I decided to continue with elements which, if not unique to being a Catholic, were at least distinctive. That is why my fourth chapter is on the rosary and the fifth chapter is about devotions. A special aspect of our Catholic faith is what we call the communion of saints, which is our relationship with people in heaven, purgatory, and on earth, so next I treated the fact that we pray for the dead, we strive to imitate the saints, and we work to live in harmony and respect with each other. I selected in particular St. Joseph and St. Vincent de Paul for reasons that are evident in the chapters which deal with them.

I felt I could not pass over the sacrament of penance since it is so characteristic of Catholics. Together we all make up the church of which Mary is the model and most eminent member, a truth I treated next. Much of our Catholicism is expressed in the gospel episode in which Jesus feeds the five thousand as I tried to show in chapter 15. All is not harmonious in the church, however, so I felt a need to treat next the topic of authentic Catholicism. I then returned to the liturgy to show that it is our great teacher. The next to last chapter is, I believe, a necessary challenge for serious Catholics to consider, and since that chapter is rather heavy, I decided to end on a note of joy.

There are many other topics that are distinctively Catholic which I have failed to treat, but I wanted this book to be brief and readable. I trust that what I have presented is without prejudice to other Christians since I have intended, not to degrade any other expression of Christianity, but only to say something helpful to Catholics.

At the end of each chapter I have suggested some questions for personal reflection by an individual or for discussion within a group.

> The Church is catholic or universal both because she possesses the fullness of Christ's presence and the means of salvation and because she has been sent out by Christ on a mission to the whole of the human race. (*The Catholic Catechism*, p. 870)

Biblical quotations are from the New Revised Standard Version. Quotations from the Second Vatican Council have been taken from the translation found in the version by Herder and Herder Association Press, New York, although in a few instances I have modified that translation by closer adherence to the original Latin. I am grateful to Father Daniel Harris, C.M., of the faculty of St. John's Seminary in the Archdiocese of Los Angeles for his expert assistance in computer technology.

I dedicate this simple work to the memory of my brother, Father Oscar Miller, C.M., who was ordained as a Vincentian priest in 1939, but who became truly a priest of the Second Vatican Council and lived and ministered in the spirit of the Council until his death on May 27, 2002.

MASS ON SUNDAY

"Do this in remembrance of me." (Luke 22:19)

In 1934 Father Leonard Feeney, S.J., wrote a book of delightful essays on being Catholic which he called *Fish on Friday*. His title referred to the law of abstinence that prohibited the eating of meat on Friday. That law was something of an external sign of our religion, faithfulness to which was a matter of pride, especially in public places. It marked people as being Catholic.

I was only four years old when Father Feeney wrote his book. I discovered and read it when I was a young seminarian at St. Vincent's High School Seminary in Cape Girardeau, Missouri in 1943. I would like to think that if Father Feeney were writing his book today, within the third millennium and after the impact of the Second Vatican Council, he would call his book *Mass on Sunday*. Since Father Feeney has long ago gone to eternal blessedness, I have seized the title for this book of essays on being Catholic.

But my book is about more than Mass on Sunday, since celebrating Mass on Sunday is not the only thing we do as Catholics, but Sunday Mass is our characteristic act. Surgeons are husbands and wives, fathers and mothers, but what they are most when they are operating is surgeons. Music conductors must perform many chores in life, just like the rest of us, but what they are most when they are directing an orchestra is conductors. And so we are most Catholic when we come together on Sunday to celebrate the Eucharist.

Father Vincent J. Donovan, a Holy Ghost Father, was a missionary to the Masai people in Tanzania for seventeen years. He says in his book, *The Church in the Midst of Creation*, that his experience taught him much about what it means to be a Catholic. Father Donovan reported that the first missionaries saw that the Masai lacked even the most basic forms of modern medicine. The missionaries built clinics, brought in medical people, mostly religious but some laypersons, and they considerably improved the health of the people. But the Masai did not become Catholics. They stuck to their old religious practices.

Next, the missionaries were convinced that the people needed education. Although the Masai were intelligent, they lacked a written language and had no means for improving themselves intellectually. The missionaries built simple schools, brought in teachers, mostly religious but some layteachers, and helped the people to develop their own language into a written form of communication. But the Masai did not become Catholics. They remained entrenched in their old ways.

Finally the missionaries built places where worship could take place with dignity. They inaugurated a form of RCIA, translated the Mass into the language of the Masai, and led the people to full, active participation in the sacred liturgy. The Masai became Catholics. The missionaries did not conclude that they should not have provided medical services for the people or that they had wasted their time in giving them the rudiments of an education. These things, they felt, had to be done, but they were not of the essence of what the missionaries had come to do. They had come to preach the good news, to call the people to faith and conversion, and to invite them into the family of the church. The missionaries had to remind themselves that it has pleased God to form us into a people who worship him in spirit and in truth. The missionaries came to realize the truth of Vatican II's teaching that "every liturgical celebration is a sacred action surpassing all others because it is an action of Christ the Priest and of his Body, the Church" (*Constitution on the Sacred Liturgy*, 7).

We do many things as Catholics but that which defines us is the celebration of the sacred liturgy, in particular the Sunday Eucharist. To put it in perhaps colloquial terms, Catholics are people who go to Mass on Sunday. To put it in the words of Pope Pius XII: "To participate in the sacred liturgy is the chief duty and supreme dignity of all Catholics" (*Mediator Dei,* 80). Finally, to put it in the words of the Second Vatican Council: "The aim to be considered above all else is the full, active, conscious, participation in the sacred liturgy by all the people since it is the indispensable source of the true Christian spirit" (*Constitution on the Sacred Liturgy,* 14).

It is no wonder that the *Constitution on the Sacred Liturgy* (43) declares: "Zeal for the promotion and restoration of the liturgy is rightly held to be a sign of the providential disposition of God in our time, as a movement of the Holy Spirit in the Church. It is today a distinguishing mark of the Church's life." We must take to heart the lesson which the missionaries in Tanzania learned: Catholics are a liturgical people.

The Mass Is Our Tradition

The Mass is our tradition. It is our way of doing things as Catholics. Tradition does mean going back to when we were young; it involves going back to the time when the church was young. Traditionally the Mass has always remained essentially the same from the time that the apostles and the earliest disciples followed the commandment which Jesus gave at the Last Supper, "Do this in memory of Me." It is our tradition.

Over the centuries the Mass has been celebrated in a multitude of languages in many different ways. Today there are four fundamental types of rites used in the celebration of Mass. They

3

are the Antiochian, the Alexandrian, the Gallican, and the Roman. The first three have never used Latin and are divided into several forms. The majority of Catholics follow the Roman rite, which first used Greek as its language but then changed to Latin in the third century and continued to use Latin until 1969. Variations throughout the centuries have not changed the essence of the Mass.

We cannot expect every Mass to be a highly emotional experience, but we should try to appreciate the significance of the Mass in our lives as Catholics. One way to arrive at this appreciation is to see that the hour of Sunday Mass is a special time during the week. Although the Mass may be seen as continuing throughout the day, and even throughout the week, there is a realistic way of perceiving that the Mass takes place within the context of a limited period of time.

When Jesus entered this world, he made holy the elements of time: days, hours, and minutes. He was born in the darkness of night; he celebrated a last supper in the evening; he died in the middle of the afternoon; he was buried before sunset; and he rose at dawn. The moment of his birth was not the moment of his death. The years of his youth were not the period of his public ministry. Even though the cross pervaded his whole life, he hung upon the cross on a certain day and for a particular period of time. The crucifixion had a beginning and it had an end. Within that span, the most momentous event in the history of the world took place.

For Jesus each moment had its own significance. For us too each moment of our life has its specific meaning. Time does nothing of itself, not even heal all wounds, but it is the condition in which "We know that all things work together for good for those who love God, who are called according to his purpose" (Rom 8:28). Time is sacred, but not all time is the same. The time of the Mass is the most precious hour of the week for us.

Even though the Mass should pervade our whole lives, it has a beginning, and it has an end.

We should resolve that we will be on time for Mass so that we may participate in its beginning. If you should arrive late for a movie, you disturb the audience but your presence or absence really makes no difference to them. The Mass begins with the gathering of the people, the sacred assembly. To arrive late for Mass is not only discourteous because it disturbs others, but it is also a failure to participate in those moments of gathering which precede the entrance of the priest and the ministers. Watching a movie is an individual experience, but participating in the Mass means becoming part of the sacred assembly and interacting with others.

If you decide to leave a movie early, you will annoy those who have to get up to let you out, but the fact that you will miss the end of the movie does not otherwise affect them. Leaving Mass early means that you have prematurely cut off your sharing prayer with people of faith. It is somewhat like a person who at a dinner might say, "I'm sorry, but I have to eat and run."

I live in Southern California where some people generally arrive late for Dodger games and leave early. I suspect they would do the same even for a World Series game. I am one of those faithful fans who wants to be there from the hopeful beginning until the happy (or sometimes bitter) conclusion. Infinitely more important to us is the hour of Sunday Mass. More important than a World Series? Infinitely more important than *anything*.

Why Should We Go to Mass?

The countries with the highest percentage of Mass attendance are, in order, the United States, Poland, and Malta. A recent poll indicated that over half the Catholics in the United States attend Mass faithfully every Sunday. I do not know how accurate that estimate is (I personally have never been questioned for any kind of poll, have you?), but it can move us to ask why we should go to Mass every Sunday. Why not just stay home? Some people say that they do not bother with church because they don't feel that they are missing anything. Others insist that they have a deeper sense of God when they are alone at the beach or in the mountains, or when they simply reflect quietly at home. I do not deny that these people really sense no lack in failing to come to church, or that they feel closer to God elsewhere. But all Catholics, both those who are regular attendees at church and those who are not, must take into consideration some very important truths.

Although God is present everywhere at all times, he has chosen to make the sacrifice of his son a reality for us only through the celebration of the Eucharist, the Mass. The real presence of Christ is the sacrament of his death and resurrection, the paschal mystery, the mystery of faith. This mystery is the central event of all human history, and so the Eucharist is the central act of our worship. The Vatican Council calls the Eucharist "the heartbeat" of the parish.

Within this sacred celebration God the Father has chosen to nourish us spiritually through word and sacrament. He gives us the gift of his Son's body and the blood, a form of nourishment which cannot be found elsewhere. And even though the scriptures can and should be read at home, they take on a special meaning within the Mass since "Christ himself speaks when the holy scriptures are read in the church" (*Constitution on the Sacred Liturgy,* 7).

The church insists that nothing can take the place of liturgical prayer, especially the Mass. The Mass is of higher value than any form of private prayer, not only because it proclaims the Word of God and celebrates the sacrament of the Eucharist, but also because it is the example and source of all authentically Christian prayer. A person who neglects the Mass can easily wander into a type of prayer which is not in harmony with the teachings of Christ and the tradition of his church. He or she runs the risk of becoming a maverick, one who is out of touch with sound doctrine and sane practice. Jesus manifests himself as the way, the truth, and the life chiefly through the liturgy, which is the indispensable source of the true Christian spirit.

The teaching of the *Constitution on the Sacred Liturgy* (7) bears repeating: "Every liturgical celebration, because it is an action of Christ the priest and of his body, the Church, is a sacred action surpassing all others. Nothing can match its claim to efficacy or equal the degree of it."

Going to Mass faithfully can even be beneficial to your health. *Time* magazine (August 1999) reported that a study done at Duke University revealed that people sixty-four years of age and older who attended weekly religious services were 46% less likely to die over a six-year period than those who went less often. No conclusions were drawn about the cause.

Catholics who do not go to Mass on Sunday are like a man and a woman who are married but who do not live together. Something essential is missing. Throughout history being a Catholic has been associated with, even identified with, the Mass. The real question is not why go to Mass, but rather, why not?

We, the people of the church, are part of a beautiful tradition which began when the Lord instituted the holy Eucharist on the night before he died, and will continue until the Lord comes again at the end of time.

Reflection and Discussion

- What are some practical means for elevating Sunday Mass as the high point of the week?

- Are there some ways in which you can make Sunday Mass more meaningful for yourself and for others?

- Try to summarize in a few words why Sunday Mass is important to you personally.

– 2 –

WHY I AM A CATHOLIC

For as often as you eat this bread and drink the cup, you proclaim the Lord's death until he comes. (1 Cor 11:26)

I count it as God's greatest grace to me that on Christmas day in 1929, two weeks after I made my appearance in this world, I was baptized into the Catholic Church. Thanks to the love of my parents I was born into their family as their son, and thanks to the love of God the Father I was born into the church as his child.

Back in the days of radio we would often hear of contests in which we were invited to send to the sponsor a statement telling in twenty-five words or less why we liked their product. I can say why I love being a Catholic in two words: the Mass.

Celebrating the Mass, the Eucharist, is what we do as Catholics. There are many other things we do, but the Eucharist, especially Sunday Eucharist, is our distinguishing mark as Catholics. I see a parallel in the great composer, Wolfgang Amadeus Mozart. Although he did many more things during a day than compose music, he was most himself when he was transforming symbols on a page, which we call notes, into magnificent compositions. It was a kind of transubstantiation. The Eucharist is like that for us.

The Eucharist is what the disciples of Jesus did from the very beginning, from that momentous night when Jesus at the Last Supper instituted the Eucharist. Throughout the centuries, whatever may have been our failures or shortcomings, we have always been faithful to the commandment of Jesus, "Do this in memory of me."

In the Eucharist we share in a wonderful tradition of God's family on this earth. I think back to the time when I was growing up in New Orleans in the 1930s. It was the time of the Great Depression but we always had food. Our family tradition was chicken on Sunday. My mother prepared it in many ways but my favorite was good old Southern fried chicken. No one complained, "What, chicken again?" We thought of chicken as a delicacy, and even more, it was a family tradition.

I found it hard to leave home and my mother's cooking, but when I was only thirteen I got on a train and traveled to Missouri to enroll in the Vincentian high school seminary. The first Sunday I was amazed to be served some kind of beef (we young seminarians called it "mystery meat"). How could it be Sunday without chicken? I began to dream about Southern fried chicken. When I returned to New Orleans for my first vacation, I had my dream fulfilled. I sat down with my family on Sunday for a Southern fried chicken dinner. I knew that I was home again.

The first disciples of Jesus felt at home in the synagogue. They were Jewish, and so for a while they continued to go to the synagogue on the Sabbath for the service which consisted of scripture readings, a homily, and prayers, but on Sunday they met in their homes to celebrate the Eucharist. When the faith spread beyond Jerusalem and Judea and from Jews to Gentiles, the essence of the synagogue service was combined with the Sunday celebration. We see this arrangement in the Liturgy of the Word joined to the Liturgy of the Eucharist.

The earliest written account of the institution of the Eucharist is found in St. Paul's First Letter to the Corinthians, which dates back to about A.D. 56. That is even earlier than the accounts found in the gospels. St. Paul reminded his converts in the eleventh chapter, verses 23–25, of this letter: For I received from the Lord what I also handed on to you, that the Lord Jesus on the night when he was betrayed took a loaf of bread, and when he had given thanks, he broke it and said, "This is my body that is for you. Do this in remembrance of me." In the same way he took the cup also, after supper, saying, "This cup is the new covenant in my blood. Do this, as often as you drink it, in remembrance of me."

Despite the clarity of the New Testament, the doctrine of the Eucharist is so extraordinary that it has not been without controversy. Just as today some people choose to deny the reality of the body and the blood of the Lord, so some people in the time of the apostles found the doctrine too hard to accept. St. John, in the fourth gospel, developing an episode from the life of Jesus, addressed the people of his era who denied the Eucharist. I suggest you take the time to read the sixth chapter of his gospel for this important presentation.

Despite controversies, Catholics have always found in the Eucharist a mark of their identity. I am particularly struck by a remarkable passage which was composed by St. Justin around A.D. 150. St. Justin was a layman and a philosopher. He wrote treatises, called apologies, to defend the Catholic faith. In one of them he explained what Catholics do on Sundays, and it is worthwhile, I believe, to quote him somewhat at length:

> On Sunday we have a common assembly of all our members. The recollections of the apostles or the writings of the prophets are read. When the reader has finished, the presider of the assembly speaks to us; he urges everyone to imitate the examples of virtue we have heard in the readings. Then we all stand together and pray. At the conclusion of our prayer, bread and wine and water are brought forward. The presider offers prayers and gives thanks, and the people give their assent by saying, "Amen." The Eucharist is distributed, everyone present com-

municates, and the deacons take it to those who are absent. The wealthy make a contribution and the presider uses it to help the orphans and the widows and all who for any reason are in distress, whether because they are sick or in prison or away from home. We hold our common assembly on Sunday because it is the first day of the week, the day on which God created the world and because on that same day our savior Jesus Christ rose from the dead.

I am awed by this passage, written as it was in the year 150, so close to the era of Christ and the apostles, and so far from our own. In St. Justin's time the Mass was celebrated in Greek. Except for the language, he would readily recognize and embrace our Mass as his own, and if we could be transported back in time we would feel right at home with him and his fellow Catholics of the second century.

In the thirteenth century the great theologian, St. Thomas Aquinas, wrote: "How wonderful the sacred banquet in which Christ is consumed, the memory of his passion is recalled, the soul is filled with grace, and the pledge of future glory is given to us" (Antiphon for the *Magnificat*, Solemnity of *Corpus Christi*). Pondering his words helps me to realize why the Eucharist is my reason for being a Catholic.

The Second Vatican Council in its *Constitution on the Sacred Liturgy* (106) gave a strong emphasis to Mass on Sunday: "By an apostolic tradition which took its origin from the very day of Christ's resurrection, the Church celebrates the paschal mystery every Sunday. On this day Christ's faithful should come together into one place so that, by hearing the Word of God and taking part in the Eucharist, they may call to mind the death and the resurrection of the Lord Jesus, and may give thanks to God."

Throughout the centuries the church has adapted the celebration of the Eucharist to circumstances and cultures, always maintaining its essence, somewhat like my mother who varied her cooking but always put chicken on the Sunday dinner table. Every Sunday we come home for the spiritual banquet Christ prepares for us. Nothing is more Catholic than God's family gathered on Sunday around the table of God's Word and the holy Eucharist. Every day I give thanks to God for the grace of being a Catholic.

Reflection and Discussion

- What is your reason for being a Catholic?

- Do you know a story about how someone became a Catholic?

- Name some distinctive elements which make the Catholic Church different from other Christian churches.

A PERSPECTIVE FOR ADORATION OF THE BLESSED SACRAMENT

"Lord, to whom can we go? You have the words of eternal life...."
(John 6:68)

A hallmark of the Catholic faith is belief in the real presence of Christ in the Blessed Sacrament. During the celebration of the eucharistic prayer, bread truly becomes the Body of Christ given up for us, and wine truly becomes his blood poured out for us. The sacramental words, "This is my body" and "This is the cup of my blood," which are spoken by Christ through the ordained priest, effect what they signify. Faith in this truth is essential to being a Catholic.

In the early church there was no devotion to the real presence preserved in a tabernacle outside of the liturgy of the Mass. The Catholic Catechism (#1370) explains that "the tabernacle was first intended for the reservation of the Eucharist in a worthy place so that it could be brought to the sick and those absent, outside of Mass." In fact, the church continues to be earnest that holy communion be available to the sick, especially to those who are about to die. Holy communion, known as Viaticum, is the sacrament to be people's spiritual nourishment on their way from this life to the next.

The Catholic Catechism goes on to explain that "as faith in the real presence of Christ in his Eucharist deepened, the Church became conscious of the meaning of silent adoration of the Lord present under the Eucharistic species." In other words, by a development of doctrine, the church began to appreciate that the real presence of Christ that is a reality within the sacrifice of the Mass continues in the consecrated bread that remains after all have received communion during Mass, and further that Christ in the Eucharist is worthy of adoration.

A proper perspective on eucharistic adoration can deepen piety and extend the effects of adoration within our lives and that of our people. The first truth is that we adore Christ in the Eucharist because he is God. He is truly divine, the only begotten Son of God the Father, equal to the Father and the Holy Spirit in all things. This great truth should make us realize that since Jesus is divine, he is everywhere. When eucharistic devotion heightens our awareness of Jesus' divinity, we leave his presence in the Eucharist to find him wherever we go. We learn to live in the presence of God, always aware that we are never alone, that Jesus is with us in every circumstance. Our lives can be full of the wonder of God all around us. This is truly a *wonder-full* way to live.

The next aspect of adoration concerns the Word of God. *The Dogmatic Constitution on Divine Revelation* (#21) declares that "the Church has always venerated the divine Scriptures, just as she venerates the Body of the Lord, since from the table of both the Word of God and of the Body of Christ she unceasingly receives and offers to the faithful the bread of life, especially in the sacred liturgy." Cardinal Ratzinger in his commentary observed that at first some of the Fathers objected to this statement since they feared that it detracted from the excellence of the real presence in the Holy Eucharist. Debate on the issue led to an appreciation of the principle that what is adored is not the *mode* of Christ's presence, but his Person. And so the statement remained. A result of this clarification has led to an understanding of the principle that in Vatican II liturgy, word and sacrament are always conjoined. Adoration of the Blessed Sacrament should follow this model of conjoining word and sacrament. It is appropriate during adoration for individuals to do *lectio divina*: the silent, reflective, and contemplative reading of sacred scripture, especially the gospels. Adoration of Christ in the Blessed Sacrament should develop a deep devotion to Christ, the Word of God, in the scriptures.

When we leave the eucharistic presence we should find Christ in everyone we meet. We become mindful of the teaching of Jesus: "Truly, I tell you just as you did it to one of the least of these who are members of my family, you did it to me" and "as you did not do it to one of the least of these, you did not do it to me." (In the liturgy before Vatican II Catholics at Mass never heard this teaching from the twenty-fifth chapter of St. Matthew's gospel. Now they hear it on the Solemnity of Christ the King in the A cycle.) We are not true in our love for Jesus if we are not true in our love for other people, indeed for all people without exception. It is related in the book, *Crossing the Threshold of Hope,* that John Paul II was asked by a reporter, "What does the pope pray for?" Without hesitation John Paul responded, "The joy and hope, the sorrow and the anxieties of the people of this age, especially of the poor or those who are afflicted in any way, are the joy and hope, the sorrow and the anxieties of the disciples of Christ since nothing that is truly human fails to raise an echo in their hearts." That response, of course, was not off the top of his head. He was quoting the opening sentence of *Gaudium et Spes (The Pastoral Constitution on the Church in the Modern World).* The spirituality of that sentence is to be nourished by true devotion to the Blessed Sacrament since the adoration of Christ in the Blessed Sacrament raises us above the individualism often characterized as the "Jesus and me" mentality.

Catholics above all must recognize that Jesus instituted the Eucharist as the sacrament of his paschal mystery, the mystery of faith, his saving death and life-giving resurrection. The real presence of Christ is the living memorial of the paschal mystery, the sacrament of the death and resurrection of Christ, the obedient response to his commandment at the Last Supper, when he instituted the Holy Eucharist, "Do this in memory of me." (To put it in scholastic terminology, the Eucharist is not *res tantum;* the Eucharist is *res et sacramentum.* The paschal mystery, the mystery of faith, is the *res tantum.*) True adoration leads to liturgical celebration since, as the church teaches, "Every liturgical celebration, because it is an action of Christ the priest and of His Body, the Church, is a sacred action surpassing all others. No other action of the Church can match its claim to efficacy nor equal the degree of it" (*Constitution on the Sacred Liturgy,* #7 and #13).

In the seminary where I teach it is easy for all of us to make short, quick visits to the Blessed Sacrament. I encourage our seminarians to take a moment for such a visit and to reflect before the time of Mass: "I am about to celebrate the holy Eucharist. What a blessing!" Or, after Mass, to reflect: "I have this day celebrated the holy Eucharist. What a blessing!" Some Catholics by a profound religious instinct are drawn to adoration of Christ in the Eucharist. This instinct should be followed since it can lead to a deep Catholic spirituality.

The purpose of eucharistic adoration is best achieved when there is a special chapel for the reservation of the Blessed Sacrament—a place where there can be peace and quiet for contemplation. We all know of instances after Mass when some of the parishioners are disturbed or upset because a group is praying the rosary aloud, or saying a novena, or someone is making the Stations of the Cross using vocal prayers. The body of the church is for public prayer, so there is a need for a quiet space for private prayer. The Blessed Sacrament chapel appropriately supplies that need. Ideally in this chapel there are no external prayers since the Catholic Catechism speaks of "silent adoration." *The General Instruction of the Roman Missal 2000* states that according to the judgment of the bishop the tabernacle is to be located either in the sanctuary apart from the altar or also in a chapel suitable for the faithful's private adoration and prayer (#315). The body of the church is for the action of the liturgy and public prayer. The chapel is for silent adoration.

Reflection and Discussion

- Can you adjust your schedule so that you can have time in the presence of the Blessed Sacrament, maybe once a week—if not for an hour, then perhaps for a half hour, or even fifteen minutes?

- How can adoration of the Blessed Sacrament help you toward a more devout celebration of the Mass?

- Try to summarize in a few words how adoration of the Blessed Sacrament can lead to a deeper appreciation of sacred scripture and a greater love for others.

– 4 –

THE ROSARY: TWENTY MYSTERIES

And he came to [Mary] and said, "Greetings favored one! The Lord is with you." (Luke 1:28)

One of our characteristics as Catholics is our devotion to the Mother of God. We fulfill her own prophecy that all generations will call her blessed. If you happen to notice that a rosary is dangling from the rear-view mirror of a car, you can be almost certain that the driver is a Catholic. Among all Catholic devotions the rosary is the most popular.

The heart of the rosary is a reflection on the twenty mysteries, encompassing the joyful, luminous, sorrowful, and glorious mysteries. It is by its nature not only an oral prayer, that consists in reciting the "Our Father" and the "Hail Mary," but also a meditative prayer. Slipping the beads through our fingers and uttering the vocal prayers should be a spiritual sedative which relieves our minds of tension and anxiety, so that we may attend to contemplative prayer.

In October 2002 Pope John Paul II added five new mysteries to the rosary to be known as "the luminous mysteries" or "the mysteries of light." The twenty mysteries begin with the incarnation, the conception of Jesus by the power of the Holy Spirit, and proceed through the life and death of Jesus to his resurrection and ascension, the sending of the Holy Spirit upon the church, and the assumption into heaven and crowning of Mary who is the model of the church. These are all the same events that we celebrate during the liturgical year. The year begins with Advent, which looks forward to those awesome events that we call the joyful mysteries of the rosary: the annunciation—the message from the angel Gabriel to Mary—followed by her visit to Elizabeth, and Mary's giving birth to the Savior. The Christmas season continues with the fourth and fifth mysteries—the presentation of Jesus in the temple as an infant, and his being found in the temple at the age of twelve after he had been lost for three days.

After Christmas and Epiphany we begin to celebrate those events which are now the mysteries of light: the baptism of Jesus, the marriage feast of Cana, the preaching of Jesus, the transfiguration, and the Last Supper. The season of Lent occupies us with the sorrowful mysteries which reach their climax in Holy Week, beginning with Palm Sunday, also called Passion Sunday since it is the Sunday for reading the passion from the gospels. Although the five sorrowful mysteries conclude with the death of Jesus on the cross, we know that his death is not an end. The sorrowful mysteries prepare us to celebrate the Sacred Triduum, the holy three days of the death, burial, and resurrection of Jesus. With Easter Sunday we enter into our liturgical observance of the glorious mysteries of the rosary. The Easter Season, which extends for fifty days until the Solemnity of Pentecost, is a time for savoring the mystery of the church, especially as seen in Mary, who is the church's excellent model in faith and love, and who in her assumption and crowning shows us our destiny as disciples of her Son, the Risen and Glorified Lord.

The Joyful Mysteries

The joyful mysteries correct two fundamental errors about Jesus. Both are extremes, and both render a proper understanding and celebration of the Mass impossible. The one asserts that

Jesus is only divine and that his humanity is imaginary or not quite real. The other maintains that Jesus is only human, that he is not really divine, only extraordinary. As we meditate on the joyful mysteries we need to see first that Mary is Jesus' link with humanity. The flesh and blood which Mary gave to her son were real. When Jesus was conceived in Mary's womb, he became human like us in all things but sin. Equally important to our meditation on the joyful mysteries is the realization that Mary conceived as a virgin by the power of the Holy Spirit. Jesus did not have a human father. His only Father is God by whom he is begotten in eternity as the Second Person of the Blessed Trinity. This truth declares that Jesus is divine, equal to his Father in all things.

When Jesus was born the angels sang "Glory to God in the highest." They anticipated the truth that every aspect of Jesus' life would give glory to God. Because of our union with Jesus at Mass we join him as he continues to offer glory to his Father. As we meditate on the fourth and fifth mysteries (the presentation and finding of Jesus in the temple), we begin to see why it is indispensable to recognize that Jesus is at once human and divine. In the fourth mystery Mary and Joseph present Jesus as an infant in the temple to God. In the fifth mystery Jesus at the age of twelve is found in the temple, his Father's house. The temple was the place of worship. In the temple of Jerusalem sacrifice was offered to God, but Jesus himself became the Lamb of God, the perfect sacrifice. He replaced both the temple and its sacrifices. Jesus was born to die. In order to be able to embrace death, the eternal Son of God had first to become human like us, since in his divinity he could not undergo death. His humanity is what made it possible for Jesus to die, but his divinity is what gave his death infinite value and significance.

When we come to Mass, we must do so with the realization that we are sharing in the death and resurrection of Jesus. We proclaim the mystery of faith: Christ has died, Christ is risen, Christ will come again. We recognize that when we eat the body of Christ and drink the cup of his blood, we proclaim the death of the Lord until he comes.

The five joyful mysteries harmonize especially with the time of Advent and Christmas, but whenever they are prayed they can help us to enter more fully into the sacred liturgy. For a better appreciation of the joyful mysteries it is very helpful to read the first two chapters of the gospel according to St. Luke.

The Mysteries of Light

When Pope John Paul II instituted the five mysteries of light (the luminous mysteries) he emphasized two elements of the rosary: the first is that it is essentially Christ-centered, and the second is that it is fundamentally a contemplative prayer. The first of these mysteries, the baptism of the Lord, marks a definitive change in the life of Jesus. For thirty years he had lived with Mary and Joseph and was their dutiful son. Now God the Father in a sense reclaimed Jesus. He declared from heaven, "You are my Son, the Beloved; with you I am well pleased" (Mark 1:11). God sent his Son into the world with a mission. Now it was time for his Son to inaugurate that mission through his teaching and preaching, and to begin those events which would lead to his death and resurrection, and his sending of the Holy Spirit upon the church. The baptism of the Lord actually is the second part of the Epiphany. The first is when Jesus was manifested (such is the meaning of the word *epiphany*) to the Magi as the Savior of the Gentiles as well as of the Jews. At his baptism, God the Father manifested Jesus as his divine Son. The baptism leads to the third part of the Epiphany which is the next mystery of light, the marriage feast of Cana. St. John in his Gospel concludes that story by saying, "Jesus did this, the first of his signs, in Cana of Galilee, and revealed [or manifested] his glory; and his disciples believed in him" (2:11).

Jesus worked the miracle of changing water into wine at the behest of Mary who represents the intercessory role of the church for God's children. The abundance of wine that Jesus supplied is a symbol of the abundance of God's love in the new covenant that, like the wine Jesus miraculously supplied, is better than the old covenant. We celebrate this new covenant when at the Eucharist the priest, speaking in the person of Christ, says over the wine, "This is the cup of my blood, the blood of the new and everlasting covenant."

Jesus then goes forth to teach about the new covenant and to preach the good news of the kingdom that we learn from the Preface for the Solemnity of Christ the King is "an eternal and universal kingdom, a kingdom of truth and life, a kingdom of holiness and grace, a kingdom of justice, love and peace." That preaching and teaching would lead to his death on the cross. To prepare his apostles for the ordeal of his passion and death, he took Peter, James, and John up a high mountain where he was transfigured before them. He showed that he had fulfilled the Old Testament, represented by Moses and Elijah, and he gave a foreshadowing of the glory that the Father would bestow upon him in the paschal mystery of his death and resurrection. And so the fourth mystery of light is the transfiguration.

On the night before he died Jesus instituted the holy Eucharist, the sacrament of the paschal mystery of his death and resurrection, the mystery of faith, the very heartbeat of our lives as Catholics. The fifth mystery is this institution of the holy Eucharist as the Last Supper. On the next day Jesus entered into his paschal mystery, the first half of which we remember as the sorrowful mysteries.

The Sorrowful Mysteries

The mysteries of the rosary are interrelated. The joyful mysteries lead to the public life of Jesus; the luminous mysteries in turn lead to the sorrowful mysteries, that lead to the glorious mysteries. Although all twenty mysteries are fulfilled in the liturgy, the sorrowful mysteries offer their special help to our participation in the Mass as the unbloody sacrifice of the cross. The paschal mystery of the death and resurrection of Jesus is one reality, but it is beneficial for us at times to concentrate on his sacrificial death. The particular benefit of meditating on the sorrowful mysteries of the rosary is that we view the sufferings and death of Jesus through the eyes of Mary. With her perspective, we should try to take on her dispositions. The suffering of Jesus was an agony for Mary. There can be no doubt about that. And yet, St. John in his Gospel is very careful to point out that Mary "stood" at the foot of the cross (19:25). The choice of the verb is deliberate. Mary did not swoon in self-pity, as we see her depicted in some misguided and mistaken forms of art. She was a devoted and loving mother who wanted to share her son's suffering, and she could not have done that if she had allowed herself to fall in a faint into the waiting arms of the beloved disciple. Her attention was so focused on Jesus that she put aside her own feelings. Mary stood in prayer. It was the posture of those who offer sacrifice. We do not know how fully Mary understood at that moment the sacrifice that was to bring salvation to the world. The gospel is silent on that point. But we can be convinced that within her heart arose the essential sentiment for offering sacrifice to God. That sentiment she had already expressed at the time of the annunciation ("Be it done to me according to your Word"), and she lived according to that sentiment all her life. Silently she prayed, "Father, your will, not mine, be done."

In reflecting on this event, Pope Pius XII, in 1943, wrote these beautiful words: "Mary, always most intimately united with her son, offered him on Calvary to the Eternal Father for all the children of Adam sin-stained by his fall, and her mother's rights and her mother's love were included in the holocaust" (*Mystici Corporis Christi*, #127).

As we meditate on the sorrowful mysteries we need to realize that at the Mass we have the privilege of standing beside Mary and following her example. United with Christ as the Head of the Body of which we are the members, we can join in the offering of his sacrifice to the Father. When Jesus was raised up on the cross, when he was "elevated," Mary stood there to share in the offering. When the body and blood of Christ are raised in the Mass, when they are elevated at the conclusion of the eucharistic prayer, we offer this life-giving bread and this saving cup in memory of his death and resurrection while we are attentive to the words of the priest: "Through him, with him, in him, in the unity of the Holy Spirit, all glory and honor is yours, almighty Father, forever and ever."

The sorrowful mysteries of the rosary are a prayerful reflection on the events which are a reality for us in the Mass. During Ordinary Time it is customary to pray the sorrowful mysteries on Tuesdays and Fridays. During the season of Lent it is appropriate to pray the sorrowful mysteries also on the other days of the week.

The Glorious Mysteries

The glorious mysteries of the rosary are arranged in a tidy balance. The first two, the resurrection and the ascension, are about Jesus, and the last two, the assumption and the crowning of Mary, are about his mother. Between them is the third mystery: the coming of the Holy Spirit to manifest the church to the world at Pentecost. This arrangement suggests that the resurrection and ascension of Jesus were more than an exaltation of his person since these events led to the manifestation of the church, the people of God, on Pentecost Sunday. In the preface of the second eucharistic prayer, the priest says, "Father...for our sake [Jesus] opened his arms on the cross; he put an end to death and revealed the resurrection. In this he fulfilled your will and won for you a holy people." Jesus opened his arms on the cross to embrace all of us and to draw us to himself, to be part of his mystical body, the church. We are those people he won for his Father and whom the Holy Spirit formed into the church.

The preeminent member of the church is Mary. She is not only the mother of Jesus she is his first and best disciple. That is why the Second Vatican Council emphasizes that Mary is a model of the church, a living sign of both what the church is and especially what it will become. In a sense, it is one thing to believe that Jesus was raised from the dead, but what about us? After all, Jesus is God; we are not. Mary helps us in that regard. Holy though she is, Mary is a human person just like us. She is not God. And yet her assumption is a sharing in the resurrection of her son. The assumption and crowning of Mary are more than an exaltation of her person. Mary is the sign that the resurrection which Jesus revealed is the destiny of the people whom he won for the Father. As we believe that Mary, after the course of her life on this earth had ended, was taken body and soul to the glory of heaven, so we have faith that we too will share in the resurrection and be brought to the fullness of life.

Pentecost and the assumption fit together. Those who are formed into the church through the gift of the Holy Spirit at Pentecost rightfully see in Mary's assumption a sign that they will share in the glory of Christ's resurrection. The glorious mysteries should help us to receive with greater faith and devotion the body and the blood of the risen Lord in holy communion. Jesus said, "Those who eat my flesh and drink my blood have eternal life, and I will raise them up on the last day" (John 6:54).

When the rosary is part of a wake service, it is appropriate to recite the glorious mysteries rather than the sorrowful. The reason is that people who have died have concluded their sharing in the sorrowful mysteries of Christ. Our prayer and our hope is that they are even now sharing in the glorious mysteries.

The Rosary in Perspective

The Second Vatican Council warmly commended devotions in honor of Mary, and urged that they harmonize with the liturgical seasons and lead the people to a fuller participation in liturgical celebrations, especially the Mass.

October is the month of the rosary. In the year 1573 Pope Pius V assigned the feast of Our Lady of the Rosary to the seventh of October. Pope John Paul II composed the following prayer to Mary: "We entrust to you the Church which acknowledges and invokes you as Mother. On earth you preceded the Church in the pilgrimage of faith: comfort her in her difficulties and trials and make her always the sign and instrument of intimate union with God and of the unity of the whole human race."

The twenty decades of the rosary invite us to join Mary "who preceded the Church in the pilgrimage of faith" by reflecting prayerfully on the life, death, and resurrection of her Son. The joyful, luminous, sorrowful, and glorious mysteries center our attention on those events which the liturgy unfolds for us within the cycle of a year—from Jesus' incarnation and birth to his resurrection and ascension and the great day of Pentecost.

The liturgy opens to us the riches of the Lord's powers and mercies by our reliving of the events of his life. These events are in some way made present to us so that we may lay hold of them and become filled with saving grace. The liturgical year comes alive for us in the degree to which we reflect prayerfully on the meaning of the incarnation, life, death, and resurrection of Jesus Christ. The rosary offers us the opportunity to meditate on these events in union with Mary and through her eyes.

The rosary helps us to celebrate the liturgical year when we allow this prayer to lead us more deeply into the meaning and beauty of the twenty mysteries. The contemplative prayer of the rosary can also alert us to the signs of these mysteries all around us. A pregnant woman reminds us of the person of Mary who was privileged to carry Jesus in her womb for nine months. Every newborn baby makes us mindful of the wonder of Christmas. A lost child helps us think of that remarkably human situation in which Jesus was lost for three days. Every lonely person turns our hearts toward Jesus during his agony in the garden, while the death of a loved one leads us to realize that even the Son of God died on the cross. Every morning's rising sun is a symbol of the resurrection of Jesus and the assumption of his mother into heaven. Hearing varied languages, whether in the street or during the Mass, makes us realize that the miracle of Pentecost continues. The reality of Christ is all around us. The rosary can help us to see it in our lives and to celebrate it in the liturgy.

All the mysteries of the life of Christ reach their fulfillment in our celebration of the holy Eucharist. The Mass is the center of our faith, the very heartbeat of the Christian community. As we meditate on the mysteries of the rosary, we ought to realize that these mysteries are present for us in the Mass.

We are to approach the rosary with serene freedom, according to the teaching of Pope Paul VI in his encyclical, *Marialis Cultus*. It should never seem to be a burden or an obligation. We need not feel that we must complete all five mysteries assigned to a given day. If we become prayerfully absorbed in a single event, the proper purpose is achieved. Nor need we think that we must scrupulously recite every "Hail Mary" without fail. The purpose of these prayers, and the feeling of the beads slipping through our fingers, is to make us realize our union with God who wishes to lead us to full, active participation in the sacred liturgy.

Although the rosary should never be said during Mass, a meditative praying of the rosary is well suited to lead us to the Mass and to the celebration of the liturgical year. The pope suggested the following arrangement: the joyful mysteries on Mondays and Saturdays, the luminous mysteries on Thursdays, the sorrowful mysteries on Tuesdays and Fridays, and the glorious mysteries on Sundays and Wednesdays.

Reflection and Discussion

- Is the rosary a favorite prayer for you? If so, explain what you like about it.

- If you find the rosary difficult to say, is there a way to benefit from its fruits without actually saying all the Our Fathers and Hail Marys?

- Think about (and discuss) ways to have the rosary lead to the celebrating of the Mass.

– 5 –

DEVOTIONS AND LITURGY

Pray without ceasing. (1 Thess 5:17)

When I was ordained in 1956, six years before the beginning of the Second Vatican Council, I was assigned to St. Vincent's Church in Los Angeles. On my first Monday morning I had the 6:30 A.M. Mass, which I offered in Latin, mostly in silence, with my back to the people. I was assisted by a little boy who sleepily struggled to get out the few Latin responses required of him.

The people said nothing aloud. Of course, since I had my back to them, I could not see what they were doing, but I supposed that, as in most places, people were saying the rosary silently, or reading from a missal or other prayer book, or simply reflecting quietly. Only a few of the small number of those present received communion. That Monday evening at 7:30 I conducted the Miraculous Medal Novena. As I entered the sanctuary the people stood, the organist hit a chord, and everyone joined rather robustly in singing *Mother Dear, O Pray for Me.* I led a number of prayers, all in English, which people recited with no little enthusiasm. We had Benediction while singing the arcane syllables of *O Salutaris* and *Tantum Ergo.* The people repeated the Divine Praises after me. We concluded with two stanzas of *Holy God, We Praise Thy Name.* There was lots of participation.

Actually matters were inverted. The Mass in the morning looked like a private devotion and the novena in the evening looked like liturgy. Because Latin was required for the liturgy, the people could not enter into full, active participation. Because English was used at the novena, they responded very well. The inversion of liturgy and devotions was gradual. Taking Rome as an example, we find that the original language there was Greek, the language of the New Testament. Anyone with even a smidgen of education understood Greek. When Latin became the language of the people, the pope (probably St. Callistus who had been a slave and was a simple man), despite opposition, primarily from a scholarly priest named Hippolytus, made the change in the early third century. But then Latin, I might say, overstayed its welcome. As people lost touch with Latin and began to speak other languages, including those which were the ancestors of modern Italian, Spanish, Portuguese, French, and German, the liturgy began to slip past both their understanding and their participation. The church had forgotten why it had changed to Latin in the first place.

To satisfy religious yearnings, something had to substitute for liturgy. That something was private devotions in the language of the people. Novenas were popular. The word, from Latin, means *nine*. The origin of novenas is the prayer for nine days between the ascension and Pentecost. St. Luke wrote that during those days the apostles "were constantly devoting themselves to prayer, together with certain women, including Mary the mother of Jesus, as well as his brothers" (Acts 1:14). Although a novena in the strict sense means nine consecutive days of prayer, the term is now used in a loose sense to mean almost any organized devotion that may occur over any period of time. When people use the prayer book of the church, the Liturgy of the Hours, they participate in the original novena between the ascension and Pentecost.

The Second Vatican Council, it should be noted, encourages devotions: "Popular devotions of the Christian people are warmly commended, provided they accord with the laws and norms of the Church" (*Constitution on the Sacred Liturgy*, 13). Devotions arise in the church to meet specific needs of the times and of the people from whom they spring. The liturgy is traditional in the sense that it was formed at the very beginning of the church and has continued throughout every era. We must remember that tradition does not go back to the time when we were young but back to the time when the church was young. The earliest disciples of Jesus, sometimes called the Jerusalem community, "devoted themselves to the apostles' teaching and fellowship, to the breaking of bread and the prayers" (Acts 2:42). "The apostles' teaching" at first consisted of the epistles, particularly the letters of St. Paul, which were read during the liturgy, but the teaching also included the oral proclamation of the life of Jesus which developed into the gospels. Their "fellowship" meant a sharing with each other as the Body of Christ. The "breaking of the bread" is the New Testament code word for the Eucharist, which was surrounded by the other sacraments. The "prayers" were the psalms, the prayer book of Israel, which became the prayer book of the first disciples and which still is the official prayer book of the church to this day. Continuing the earliest prayer life of the church, the liturgy comprises the seven sacraments and the Liturgy of the Hours that are celebrated and experienced within the liturgical year. The liturgy is enduring [and should be endearing as well] in the sense that it is the church's "official" worship of God in every age of the church and in every place. We continue in our time and in our way to devote ourselves to the apostles' teaching, to fellowship, to the breaking of the bread, and to prayers.

The Stations of the Cross

We need devotions to supplement the liturgy. My favorite devotion (at least at this time, but I reserve the right to change my mind as I grow older) is the Stations of the Cross. This devotion in its original form was the first devotion in the church. St. Jerome and others attest to the fact that Catholics in the earliest centuries made pilgrimages to Jerusalem so that they could prayerfully visit the scenes of Jesus' passion and death on what is called the *Via Dolorosa.*

The first stations to be arranged in a coherent sequence outside of Palestine were in the Church of St. Stefano in Bologna in the fifth century. During the twelfth and thirteenth centuries, devotion to the passion became widespread. Then in the eighteenth century St. Leonard of Port Maurice, known as the preacher of the Way of the Cross, promoted the devotion in an extraordinary manner. It is said that he erected more than 572 sets of stations between 1731 and 1771. There have been variations in the number of the stations over the centuries, but the devotion was stabilized by Pope Clement in 1731. It has often been observed that the present fourteen stations are incomplete without a consideration of the resurrection, and it has been suggested that a fifteenth station be added. Of course the liturgy of the Eucharist constantly reminds us that the death of Jesus led to his resurrection.

The Stations of the Cross complement the liturgy which, following the message of the four gospels, celebrates the meaning of the death and resurrection of Jesus, not its circumstances. The gospels are stark in their narrative. Even St. Mark, who is characterized by an emphasis on vivid details in his Gospel, says simply, "They crucified him, and divided his clothes among them, casting lots to decide what each should take" (15:24). The gospels give us no detailed description of the extent of Jesus' suffering. The reality is that Jesus was human like us in all things but sin. His sufferings were real and intense. Devotion that is imbued with the meaning of the incarnations fills up what is lacking in the scriptural presentation and liturgical celebration of the passion. That kind of devotion helps us to enter into the human character of the passion. That is why I favor the Stations of the Cross.

On Good Friday the pope, according to an old tradition, leads people in the Stations of the Cross at the Colosseum in Rome. In 1991, Pope John Paul II introduced a new format and added a fifteenth station for the resurrection. The new format is as follows: I. Jesus prays in the garden. II. Jesus is betrayed and arrested. III. Jesus is condemned by the Sanhedrin. IV. Peter denies knowing Jesus. V. Jesus is condemned by Pilate. VI. Jesus is scourged and crowned with thorns. VII. Jesus takes up his cross. VIII. Simon of Cyrene helps Jesus. IX. Jesus meets the weeping women. X. Jesus is crucified. XI. Jesus promises paradise to the crucified thief. XII. Jesus cares for his mother. XIII. Jesus dies. XIV. Jesus is buried. XV. Jesus is raised from the dead. Missing from this version is the customary fourth station that depicts Jesus' meeting his mother on the way to the cross. Also missing is the sixth station where Veronica wipes the face of Jesus. Actually, neither of these episodes is recorded in the gospels. The new version does not mention the three falls of Jesus. My limited experience is that in the parishes I'm familiar with, the community has followed the customary stations, which is entirely permissible. Personally, I like the old way mainly because I know the sequence by heart, and at times I make the stations in my mind when I go for my daily walk.

I love the community aspect of liturgy and the family character of our worship, but some devotions are best followed in solitude. Although it is beneficial for a parish or other community to make the stations together, especially during Lent, my personal preference is to make this meditation alone. I want to save the energy it takes to be active in community for the celebration of the liturgy. Also every now and then I find myself spending so much time in reflecting on one of the stations that I do not have the opportunity to complete all fourteen. The stations are a contemplative devotion. No oral prayers are necessary, only devout reflection. Every Catholic church is to have the fourteen stations, but anyone can fulfill the purpose of this devotion anywhere and at any time.

Other Forms of Devotions

Of course there are many forms of devotions in the church in addition to the stations. The measure of the appropriateness of any devotion is an affirmative answer to three questions: Is the devotion in accord with the teachings of the church? Does the devotion at least in some way derive from the liturgy of the church? Does the devotion lead participants to a full, active participation in the liturgy? An affirmative answer to all three questions is necessary to establish that a devotion is proper and correct for Catholics.

There is a growing appreciation of the ancient practice known in Latin as *lectio divina* (which literally means "divine reading," but it is one of those expressions which should simply be part of our Catholic vocabulary without a literal translation). It consists in a reflective reading of sacred scripture. There are no strict rules, but a usual method is to begin by reading slowly, very deliberately, a passage from the Bible (most people like to concentrate on the gospels). (I usually read the text aloud, to hear the words, to savor their meaning.) As soon as you are struck by something in the text (it may be a single word, or a phrase, or a paragraph), stop reading and reflect on the meaning. Allow your reflection to be lifted up to prayer for a deeper understanding so that the meaning may become part of your life. Prayer can then lead to a contemplative spirit so that you rest in a wordless sense of oneness with God. After a while you may pick up the Bible again and repeat the process for as long as you have the time. The steps are: read, reflect, pray, contemplate. I think it is most appropriate to read the scriptures for the following Sunday, or if you attend Mass every day, it is helpful to set aside some time in the evening to read the scriptures for the next day (both Sunday and daily missals are available in Catholic bookstores). The scriptures are a precious gift from God. Their value should move us to set aside time from other activities for the sake of *lectio divina*.

Contemplation, whether it follows the model of *lectio divina* or not, is a key form of devotion which unlocks the door to the treasures of the spiritual life. We need to think about the meaning of our faith, to ponder the meaning of life, to discern what God's plan is for us, to examine our relationship with people, and above all to fix our gaze on the person of Jesus as he is presented in the scriptures and the other teachings of the church. All of that, if I may be so bold as to insist, is more important than following external devotions. To be serious about being a Catholic requires time and energy that we may have to take from other activities. The pagan philosopher, Socrates, said that the unexamined life is not worth living. The saints have been convinced that no price is too high for deepening our relationship with God and each other.

No devotion is indispensable to the life of the church. Only the liturgy is essential. Catholics should, however, continue to follow approved devotions according to their needs or choices, but all of us, with great gratitude to the Second Vatican Council for its providential changes, must enter enthusiastically into the indispensable source of the true Christian spirit—full, active participation in the liturgy.

Reflection and Discussion

- What is your favorite devotion and why?

- Does "contemplation" seem so profound that you believe it is suited only for very holy people?

- How can we overcome distractions in a busy, noisy world to make time for a life that includes devotions?

– 6 –

WHY CATHOLICS PRAY
FOR THE DEAD

It is a holy and pious thought to pray for the dead. (2 Macc 12:45)

A politician died, so the story goes, and his wife put a notice in the obituary column which read: "Los Angeles: today my husband, Willoughby Dubius, departed for heaven at 3:30 A.M." The next day a notice appeared in the paper: "Heaven: 8:30 P.M. Mr. Dubius has not yet arrived. Whereabouts unknown."

Perhaps whoever put the second notice in the paper, although wishing to be humorous, needed to be patient. Nowhere in scripture, or the other teachings of the church, do we find any doctrine which declares that we are static after death, that death immediately means either heaven or hell. Even after death God gives us the opportunity to grow in his grace, to overcome our selfishness, and to become better suited to enjoy the blessedness of heaven.

I think we can all acknowledge that when we have concluded life in this world we are probably not quite good enough to go directly to heaven, but surely not bad enough to go to hell. Does that mean we must remain in some nebulous condition, suspended as it were between the state of paradise and that of perdition? Those who believe in God's mercy can give a resounding "No" to that question. God applies to us the reconciling grace of his Son's sacrificial death as we pass through a state of purification when "we are washed clean in the blood of the Lamb." We call that state purgatory.

The teaching of our faith is that despite our imperfections, we need not despair. Purgatory is a hope-filled reality. It is not so much a punishment as it is an opportunity for spiritual maturation. It is a grace from God by which we are purged of that self-ishness which prevents us from becoming one with God. In the moment of death, life for God's faithful people is changed, not ended. This means that spiritual growth is still possible after death, provided that we have not turned our backs on God but have made a final choice to embrace him. The suffering or pain of purgatory is that which is involved in surrendering our ego-centered selves so that we may become completely centered on God. Sometimes parents tell little children who complain of aching muscles that they are having "growing pains." Purgatory could be called *spiritual* growing pains.

Should we pray for the dead? People who are in need, people who are out of work, or who are going into the hospital for surgery, ask for our prayers. In charity we must be willing to offer prayers for others. This Christian obligation of loving concern does not cease with death, and neither does the possibility of fulfilling it. In praying for the dead, we can find a great consolation when we realize that such prayer is an expression before God of our love for those who have gone before us in death.

God echoes our prayers to those for whom we pray. He makes them hear our words of affection and love, words which perhaps during life we said too infrequently or with too little feeling. As death is not the end of growth for those who have died, so it is not the end of our opportunity to manifest and to increase our love for a deceased parent, a spouse, a child, a friend, or even an enemy.

We pray for the dead in purgatory just as we pray for each other on this earth. We help each other by means of prayer, and we help those who have gone before us in death in the same way. St. Monica, on her death bed, said to her son St. Augustine, a bishop: "One thing only I ask of you, that you remember me at the altar of the Lord wherever you may be."

Two great liturgical observances, those of All Saints' Day and All Souls' Day, remind us that we are united with those who have gone before us in death, both those in heaven and those temporarily in purgatory. The saints in heaven pray for us, the church on earth. We in turn pray for those who have left this earth but are still on the journey to their true home in heaven.

It is always sad to endure the death of a loved one, but one of the saddest stories I was ever told was from a woman who had just lost her mother. A "friend" sent her a condolence card in which she wrote, "I will pray for you but not for your mother. It is not right to pray for the dead." The bereaved woman did not know which she felt the most—shock or dismay!

Some of those who don't believe in praying for the dead appeal to the mantra, "Jesus is my personal Lord and Savior," or "We are saved by faith alone." Catholics are then challenged to find a passage in scripture which supports prayers for the dead. In the Second Book of Maccabees (12:45–46), we find this beautiful statement: "It is a holy and wholesome thought to pray for the dead that they may be released from their sins." But we ought to realize that we need not necessarily make an appeal to scripture, since the opinion that scripture alone is the source of doctrine is an impossible stance and therefore an erroneous view. By a constant tradition the church has always prayed for the dead. That tradition is the foundation of our practice today. In every Mass, during the eucharistic prayer we offer intercessions for the dead. We pray: "Bring all the departed into the light of his presence" (second eucharistic prayer). We pray: "Welcome into your kingdom our departed brothers and sisters and all who have left this world in your friendship" (third prayer). We pray:

"Remember those who have died in the peace of Christ and all the dead whose faith is known to you alone." (fourth prayer).

Each year on the second of November we are invited, even urged, to pray fervently for the dead. When possible we should participate in the highest form of prayer, the Mass. Although death seems to be a separation, it does not make us lose contact with those who have gone before us. We are united with them through the communion of saints. Our voices raised in prayer are their voices before God; our hands lifted in prayer are their hands lifted up to God; for we form one body, one spirit, in Christ.

In the Mass of All Souls' Day, after communion we pray: "Lord God, may the death and resurrection of Christ which we celebrate in the Eucharist bring the departed faithful to the peace of your eternal home." Prayer for the dead is one of the most beautiful aspects of our Catholic faith. The older I get, and the more I see loved ones preceding me in death, the more I appreciate the opportunity God graciously grants us to pray for the dead.

The *Catechism of the Catholic Church* says of purgatory in its glossary that purgatory is "a state of final purification after death and before entrance into heaven for those who died in God's friendship but were only imperfectly purified." Some people may not want me to pray for them after they have died, but I personally will take all the prayers I can get when I have departed from this life. What a mistake it is to think that prayer for the dead is useless or inappropriate! Praying for the dead is one of the most edifying traditions of our Catholic faith.

Reflection and Discussion

- Think about friends and relatives who have gone before you in death. Name as many as you can. Plan ways to pray for them regularly.

- Think about how you can heal what was a bad relationship with someone who has died.

- Try to think about how you can make prayers for the dead part of your daily prayers.

CATHOLICS
AND THE SAINTS

...I looked, and there was a great multitude that no one could count, from every nation, from all tribes and peoples and languages.... (Rev 7:9)

One of our distinctive characteristics as Catholics is our devotion to the saints. We set aside days to honor them in the liturgy, and in every Mass during the eucharistic prayer we remember Mary, the apostles, and all the saints. So that no saint may be forgotten, we even have a special feast of All Saints on the first day of November.

We live in the communion of saints. This beautiful doctrine tells us that we are all interrelated, not only with each other on this earth but even with those who have gone before us in faith. Because of the communion of saints, we can pray for each other on this earth and we benefit by the prayers of those in heaven.

Two people who are examples of our communion with each other on this earth are Monica and her son, Augustine. These two saints manifest for us the power of prayer, especially the prayer of concern for the good of those whom we love. In his youth Augustine was a personification of the prodigal son, and caused his devout mother much grief. Like the father in the parable, Monica did not give up on her wayward son, even though he led a dissolute life and adhered to a pagan-like religion, Manichaeism.

Monica prayed fervently for the conversion of her son. Her prayers were answered in an extraordinary way. Augustine abandoned his old style of life and was baptized. He later was ordained a bishop, developed into the outstanding theologian of his era, and became a great saint. Augustine attributed his conversion to the prayers of his mother, a conviction which influenced his thinking on the power of prayer. Augustine found an example of that power in the martyrdom of St. Stephen as related in the Acts of the Apostles. Saul (who was later to be known as Paul) held the cloaks of those who were stoning Stephen. He concurred in the act of killing. Stephen, while he was being stoned to death, prayed for his persecutors. Augustine's reflection on this event led him to believe that if "Stephen had not prayed, the Church would not have had St. Paul." Despite his strong language, Augustine would of course be quick to affirm that God may act in any way he chooses and is surely free to grant his grace whether we pray for others or not. And yet Augustine was convinced that the prayers of St. Stephen were instrumental in the conversion of Paul and that the prayers of his mother helped to change his own life.

We all have people we want to pray for. Almost every family has some members who have become alienated from the church or who simply no longer practice their faith. We have friends who were baptized Catholics and who have either gone over to some other religion or who profess no religion at all. The example of St. Monica and the conversion of St. Augustine motivate us to be fervent in prayer for these people. The best time for this prayer is during the Mass, especially within the Prayer of the Faithful. Almost every parish allows time for silent petitions during the Sunday Mass, and on weekdays may even accept voiced petitions. Love for others and faith in the power of prayer should motivate us to want to pray for the conversion and reconciliation of those who are in need. Monica and Augustine help us focus on prayers for conversion, but of course we pray for each other according to other intentions as well. Many of the requests I receive for prayer are for good health, for overcoming a disease, for a successful operation. Faith in the power of prayer is one of the gifts which come to us through our devotion to the saints.

We must imitate the saints not only in our prayers of intercession, but in every way. We come to realize what it means to imitate the saints when we recognize how they have become saints. They are not self-made people; they are God-made. They become saints by God's grace with which they cooperate. They became like Christ who is the model of perfect holiness. God the Father's plan for all of us is that we should become conformed to the image of his Son, to be God's children as Jesus is God's unique Son. St. John wrote, "See what love the Father has bestowed on us in letting us be called children of God! Yet that is what we are." But not all saints are the same. Since no saint can possibly reflect all the wonder which is Jesus Christ, each saint tends to specialize in one of his characteristics. Examples are rather easy to think of. St. Francis of Assisi was the man of poverty. He reflects Jesus who was so poor that in his missionary journeys he had no place to lay his head. St. Teresa of Avila was a mystic and is recognized by the Church as a Doctor of Prayer. She was like Jesus who went off and spent whole nights in prayer. St. John Chrysostom, the patron of preachers, continued the mission of Jesus who declared that he was sent by the Father to preach the good news to the poor. St. Vincent de Paul was like Christ in his great concern and affection for the needy and the outcasts of society. St. John of the Cross was true to his title and like Jesus endured great suffering for God. St. Damien "the leper" was like Jesus who reached out to touch and cure those who were afflicted with the most feared disease of his time.

The saints tell us that it can be done. Mere human beings can by the grace of God become holy. The saints in heaven are not few in number. They are "a huge crowd which no one can count from every nation, race, people, and tongue." They "have washed their robes and made them white in the blood of the lamb" through the sacrament of baptism. So have we. This great sacrament is our initial conformity to Christ. It makes us children of God and heirs of heaven. It is the beginning of our journey on the way to holiness. We, like the many women, men, and children who have gone before us in faith, can become saints. We should never minimize the reality of God's call nor underestimate the power of his grace.

A young woman died at the age of twenty-four. She had never traveled from her home in a small French village, except once when her father took her to Rome at the age of sixteen. She was not a great missionary. She was not a martyr. In fact, she did nothing at all that seemed extraordinary. And yet she is *Saint Thérèse* of Lisieux, the "Little Flower." How did it happen? She determined to do everything, even the most insignificant thing, out of pure love for God. It was her way, her "little way" of spiritual childhood. She was a child of God who became like the Son of God in her simplicity.

What is *our* way? How are we to live like Christ? We must determine that for ourselves. But we must remember that saints are not self-made. Our power comes from the holy Eucharist. When we receive the body and blood of the Lord, we receive the grace to become like Christ, each one of us in our own distinctive way. St. Francis de Sales, in his wonderful little book *Introduction to a Devout Life,* teaches that there is no one way to become a saint. He insists that it is absurd, for example, to think that parents of little children should be as unconcerned about money as a cloistered nun, or that a working person should spend as much time in church as a monk. And yet, there is a fundamental spirituality which is necessary for every form of sanctity, and that fundamental spirituality is exemplified by St. John Gabriel Perboyre, a French Vincentian priest who was martyred in 1840.

When John Gabriel was ordained, he asked to be sent to China as a missionary but was told he was to teach in a seminary. Meanwhile his older brother, also a Vincentian priest, had been assigned to the mission in China but died on board ship before reaching his destination. When John Gabriel heard of his brother's death, he begged his superiors to allow him to take his brother's place in the mission. They granted him permission. The young priest was very successful in making converts and had developed a rather large Catholic community when a terrible persecution broke out. The Chinese government was determined to expel all foreigners, especially priests and sisters. John Gabriel, rather than abandon his community, went into hiding with a number of them, until he was betrayed to the Chinese officials by one of his own converts. He was arrested, dragged from one tribunal to another, and finally condemned to death. He was led out on a Friday afternoon to a hill where, tied to a cross, he was strangled to death. Pope Leo XIII, in beatifying John Gabriel Perboyre, remarked on the striking similarity between the passion and death of Jesus and that of this priest.

After John Gabriel's death, some of his followers found this handwritten prayer in his room.

O my divine Savior, transform me into yourself. May my hands be the hands of Jesus. May my tongue be the tongue of Jesus. Grant that every faculty of my body may serve only to glorify you. Above all transform my soul and all its powers that my memory, my will, and my affections may be the memory, the will, and the affections of Jesus. I pray you to destroy in me all that is not of you. Grant that I may live but in you and by you and for you, and that I may truly say with St. Paul, "I live, now not I, but Christ lives in me."

John Gabriel Perboyre was declared a saint by Pope John Paul II on Trinity Sunday, June 2, 1996. His prayer lifts us up to the essential disposition for being a saint: conformity to Christ. When we come to Mass, we have before us the chief means for growth in holiness: the sacrament of the holy Eucharist. In giving us his body and blood, Christ wants to draw us into communion with himself. Living in accord with our oneness with Christ leads us into God's kingdom of holiness. I find the prayer of St. John Gabriel an expression of just what our disposition should be after receiving holy communion, since holy communion is meant to be a sacrament of transformation.

In the New Testament era all living Christians were afforded the title of saint. They were a "chosen race, a royal priesthood, a holy nation" (1 Pet 2:9). When persecutions raged against the church, it became obvious that some Christians were heroic by persevering in their faith despite threats, torture, and even death itself. The name of "saint" began to be reserved for martyrs. But when persecutions ended, the church broadened its vision of how people live the Christian life. It saw that dedicated Christians exemplify not only Christ's death, but all aspects of his life: his preaching, his intense prayer, his healing ministry to the sick, his love and concern for all classes of people, especially children and the poor.

For centuries the people of the church gave the recognition of sainthood by acclamation. After the death of someone who seemed to have lived a life of intense union with Christ, the voice of the people declared that person to be a saint. Eventually an elaborate process, known as canonization, developed for determining who deserved official recognition as a person of extraordinary holiness. Now the church is very careful that the person proposed for sainthood is truly worthy.

One unhappy effect of the canonization process is that it tends to scare us away from any serious thought of becoming a saint. We feel we are not worthy of such aspirations and that sainthood is simply too much to hope for. You can even hear some people say, "I will be happy just to make it into purgatory." The Solemnity of All Saints helps us to adjust our thinking. Although Mary and Joseph, the apostles and martyrs and the great saints, such as Francis of Assisi and Thérèse of Lisieux, are part of the celebration, this is really a special day for the "little" saints as well—ordinary people who were never formally canonized by the church, but who tried to live according to God's will, as we are doing. These are the people whom Jesus declares are mother, brother, and sister to him.

The saints show us two important aspects of our faith. The first is that we are to pray for each other. That is a conclusion from our doctrine of the communion of saints. The second is that through, with, and in Christ we can all become truly holy.

Reflection and Discussion

- Who is your favorite saint? Describe what is so appealing to you about this saint?

- Are there other saints to whom you have devotion?

- Think about (and discuss) how All Saints' Day can be more meaningful to you.

−8−

PUTTING ST. JOSEPH
IN HIS PLACE

"...Joseph, Son of David, do not be afraid to take Mary as your wife...." (Matt 1:20)

Pope John XXIII, to the surprise of most and the chagrin of some, convoked the Second Vatican Council in 1962. He simplified the missal of Pope St. Pius V (the "Tridentine Mass") and added the name of Joseph to the Roman Canon. These days we would judge his actions to have been modest, but in his era these moves were bold indeed. Before my ordination in 1956, as I was learning the rubrics of the Mass, our professor warned us that to change a single word in the Roman Canon constituted a mortal sin, the prayer in its Latin form being considered that sacred.

Pope John considered the name of Joseph sacred enough to be included in the Canon. At the time the Roman Canon was the only eucharistic prayer in our Western liturgy. I do not think we are amiss in concluding that had he lived beyond the time of the Council, Pope John would have directed that the name of Joseph be included in all of the eucharistic prayers which have been added to our liturgy, so that the name of Joseph would in every instance be linked with that of Mary, the Mother of God.

God himself chose Joseph to be Mary's husband. It was truly a "marriage made in heaven." At first Joseph was not comfortable about his role, but he was assured by the angel that he was not to divorce Mary. And yet in many, perhaps most, of our churches we place the stature of Mary to one side and Joseph far away on the other side as if Joseph had carried out the divorce. The Preface for the Solemnity of St. Joseph beautifully proclaims: "With a husband's love he cherished Mary, the virgin Mother of God." At least in our eucharistic prayers Mary should not be separated from the man whom God chose to be her husband. That is the first reason for including Joseph.

A second reason for including Joseph in every eucharistic prayer stems from the role which God gave Joseph in his relationship with Jesus. Again the Preface for the Solemnity of St. Joseph proclaims: "He is that just man, that wise and loyal servant, whom you placed at the head of your family. With fatherly care he watched over Jesus Christ your Son, conceived by the power of the Holy Spirit." Joseph is at times called a "foster father," but that does not diminish his importance to Jesus. In the Jewish home in Nazareth in which Jesus grew up, Joseph, whom God had placed at the head of the family, was the rabbi, the teacher. Most of us learned our prayers and much of our faith from our mothers. Joseph fulfilled that role for Jesus. When other families gathered with Mary and Joseph to celebrate the Passover supper, Jesus took great pride when it was his turn as the youngest child to fulfill a special role at the beginning of the supper. He looked intently into the eyes of Joseph and asked the question, "Father, why is this night different from every other night?" Then Jesus heard this man to whom he gladly offered the love of a son present the ancient story of the Exodus, how God had led his ancestors out of slavery in Egypt into the freedom of the People of God. Would not Jesus be pleased for us to include the name of Joseph in the prayer which celebrates our Christian Passover which Jesus accomplished to free us from sin and to form us into his mystical body, the church?

There are more reasons for honoring Joseph. Jesus learned much from Joseph. When he saw Joseph at work in his carpenter's shop, Jesus came to recognize the value and dignity of human labor. He experienced in Joseph the meaning of the beatitudes before he preached them: he loved Joseph as the man who was blessed in being poor, meek, and single-hearted. From Joseph he also came to appreciate the importance of following the liturgical customs of his people.

During his public ministry of teaching and preaching, Jesus constantly proclaimed the love of God his Father. I believe that for his mission, Jesus had Joseph in his mind as a human model for his heavenly Father. When Jesus taught us to pray, he addressed God with the same word he lovingly spoke again and again to Joseph, *Abba!* The affection he felt for his earthly *Abba* reflected his devotion to his heavenly *Abba*. Jesus, I believe, remembered how Joseph had provided for him and Mary when he asked who would give [his] child a snake if the child asked for a fish (see Matt 7:10). When Jesus verbally painted the picture of the father who embraced his prodigal son, could he not have been remembering that Joseph hugged him tightly when as still a young boy he was found after three days in the temple?

On the Sunday after Christmas we celebrate the feast of the Holy Family. A family is made up of at least three persons: father, mother, and child. Or is it? These days we speak of "one-parent families," and that one parent in most cases is a mother. Where is the father? Even in some two-parent families, the kids at times must ask, "Where is dad?" Recognizing that generalizations admit of admirable exceptions, many people observe that we have lost something in our society regarding the beneficial effects of a loving and devoted father within a family. A loving, masculine influence tends to be lacking. Boys find a male role model outside the family, often in objectionable ways. No matter how dedicated a woman is, she should never be expected to be both mother and father to her children.

From the gospel story of the conception, birth, and childhood of Jesus there emerges this quiet, modest figure who is the perfect model for fathers today. St. Bernardine of Siena (early fifteenth century) said in a sermon: "What then is Joseph's position in the whole Church of Christ? Is he not a man chosen and set apart? Through him and, yes, under him Christ was fittingly and honorably introduced into the world."

We Catholics have always prided ourselves on devotion to Mary, the Mother of God. I personally feel that she would be delighted to see us deepening our devotion to her husband. Jesus would be pleased more than anyone. With Jesus we owe honor to Joseph, and honored indeed would Joseph be if fathers were to accept him as their model. Perhaps adding Joseph to every eucharistic prayer is the emphasis needed to make fathers more aware of him as their model.

St. Bernardine also said in his sermon (see the Office of Readings in the Liturgy of the Hours on his memorial): "Jesus does not now deny to Joseph the intimacy, reverence, and very high honor which he gave him on earth as a son to his father." It is appropriate that in every eucharistic prayer we not deny to Joseph this same sense of intimacy, reverence, and very high honor and so be led to cherish Joseph as did Jesus himself.

Reflection and Discussion

- How is St. Joseph a model for fathers?

- How is St. Joseph a model for husbands?

- How is St. Joseph a model for all of us?

VINCENT DE PAUL: A SAINT FOR OUR TIMES

"...he has anointed me to bring good news to the poor."
(Luke 4:18)

St. Vincent de Paul died on September 27, 1660 in his eightieth year of life, almost three and a half centuries ago, and yet he is a saint for our times and a priest in the spirit of the Second Vatican Council. Some people say that if you want something done right, you have to do it yourself. St. Vincent believed that if you want to do something right in the church, get others involved. His plan was: organize, motivate, activate. He acted in the apostolate in accord with the Vatican II principles of subsidiarity and collaboration.

As a young priest Vincent needed a conversion from an outlook characterized by not a little greed and individualism. Once God's grace took hold of him and moved him to develop an unselfish love for the poor, nothing could deter him. When he was made pastor in the little French town of Chatillon, he saw a great need among most of his people. He gathered a group of six women whom he called the "Confraternity of Charity." They were to be the servants of the poor. It was his first effort at organizing people for the apostolate and he continued that effort at every opportunity. As the numbers of the Confraternities increased he saw the need for someone to visit and direct them. He gratefully accepted the services of a widow,

Louise de Marillac, with whom he would establish the Daughters of Charity.

When he moved to Paris he realized that women who passed their days in leisure could become apostles of compassion. He motivated them to be generous to the poor, and he organized them as the Ladies of Charity. Vincent was a realist; he understood that these ladies of the aristocracy and the upper class could not be expected in that era to prepare food for the poor and go to the garrets where they lived. He saw the importance of engaging the help of a few good-hearted young women who could cooperate with the Ladies. One day Vincent met a young girl who had come from the country to Paris. She was just the kind of person he was looking for. Her name was Marguerite Naseau. She became the first Daughter of Charity, the first of many who would respond to the call to serve God's poor, especially the sick poor, in a practical manner. The Daughters of Charity today number over 25,000 throughout the world.

Vincent was not only an organizer but a great preacher who, contrary to the pomposity in the pulpits of the day, spoke to the people in a simple, familiar style as had Jesus himself. Again his spirit of collaboration made him realize that the priestly mission to the poor was not something for him to do by himself, and so he embraced a small group of zealous priests whom he called officially the "Congregation of the Mission," but he preferred his affectionate title of the "Little Company." His priests, together with lay brothers, were to serve the poor and to form other priests for pastoral ministry. Today they are known as the Vincentians and number about four thousand.

Vincent is a saint for the era of the Second Vatican Council. Before Vatican II, ministry was a vocation for priests and religious almost exclusively, but the Council recognized that we all form the church and that we are all called to ministry. We sometimes say that necessity is the mother of invention. When our developing economy in the early part of the twentieth century needed many inexpensive automobiles, Henry Ford invented the assembly line to serve that purpose (although with detriment to human dignity). In the church necessity has been the mother, not of invention, but of discovery. The need for lay people to fill up what was lacking in ministry because of the shortage of priests and religious has led us to discover the importance of lay ministers in the church (to the enhancement of their dignity). Even if some day we suddenly find ourselves with very many vocations to the priesthood and religious life, we must never return to an earlier era in which the laity were almost entirely passive. The church is the Body of Christ and all the members are called to fulfill their role.

The nature of the church is manifested in the liturgy. In fact, the *Constitution on the Sacred Liturgy* in its second paragraph declares that "the liturgy is the outstanding means by which the faithful can express in their lives and manifest to others the mystery of Christ and the real nature of the true Church." In the manner of offering the Mass which was the norm before Vatican II, the priest did everything himself because outside the liturgy nothing was considered truly Catholic unless a priest, or on occasion a religious, did it. The church is now eager to lead everyone in the church to full, active participation in the liturgy as well as to full, active participation in the apostolate of the church. The liturgy manifests that the church is the body of Christ, composed of diverse members, each with an important ministry. There are lay lectors at Mass, not because the priest is incapable of reading, but because the proclamation of the Word is a ministry fulfilled in the church by lay catechists and other teachers. There are servers at Mass, not to make things convenient for the priest, but because lay people in the church serve and assist the poor, the shut-ins, and the homeless. There are ministers of holy communion, not because distributing communion would take too long without them, but because lay people help to nourish the hungry. There are ushers, who are perhaps better named as ministers of hospitality, not simply to help seat people at Mass, but because the members of the church must welcome everyone to God's house and the table of the Lord. Liturgical ministers need not be the same ministers who serve outside the liturgy, but they do manifest that the church through its members is committed to ministry in society.

Some seem to have the idea that the only reason for ministers in the church, both outside and within the liturgy, is that we do not have enough priests. For example, they stress that lay ministers of holy communion are "extraordinary" ministers only, and that they should be employed in only the most unusual circumstances. Actually the English word *extraordinary* is not a correct translation of the Latin *extraordinarius*. The Latin term means "not by office," but by deputation. In 1973 the Bishops' Committee on the Liturgy asked that we refer to the laity who have been deputed to distribute holy communion as "special" ministers, not "extraordinary" ministers. The real point at issue, however, is that those who want to make all lay ministry, whether liturgical or apostolic, merely a substitute for insufficient numbers in the clergy, are acting from an ecclesiology, an approach to the church, which is different from that of the Second Vatican Council. At a jubilee Mass dedicated to the laity on November 26, 2000, Pope John Paul II said: "With the council, the hour of the laity in the Church truly struck." St. Vincent lived the vision of the Second Vatican Council centuries before the Council was even a dream in the mind of Pope John XXIII. St. Vincent shows us the way to organize, to motivate, to activate. He lived the meaning of collaboration and subsidiarity.

The International Vincentian Family is composed not only of those groups whom Vincent founded directly during his lifetime, but also of others who have been activated by his ideals. Among these are the Federation of the Sisters of Charity of St. Vincent de Paul (founded in 1734), the Sisters of Charity Federation in the Vincentian-Setonian Tradition (founded in

1809 by St. Elizabeth Ann Seton), the Society of St. Vincent de Paul (founded by Blessed Frederick Ozanam and some of his college classmates in 1833), the Religious of St. Vincent de Paul (founded in 1845), the Vincentian Marian Youth (founded in 1847), and the Association of the Miraculous Medal (founded in 1905).

Vincent is truly a saint for our times. He is not dead. He lives not only in heaven, enjoying the splendor of the messianic banquet, surrounded by his beloved poor, but also in the people of the church who are inspired by his charism of charity in accord with the church of the Second Vatican Council.

Reflection and Discussion

- What do you know about St. Vincent beyond what is found in this chapter?

- Do you see the spirit of St. Vincent anywhere in your parish or in your experience?

- Think about going to a Catholic bookstore and looking for a book on St. Vincent.

– 1 0 –

PEOPLE ARE SACRED

You are a chosen race, a royal priesthood, a holy nation, God's own people.... (1 Pet 2:9)

When I was ordained in 1956 I was first appointed to St. Vincent's Church in Los Angeles while I was taking classes at the University of Southern California (walking distance from St. Vincent's). Rather frequently I was assigned to the 6:30 A.M. Mass for the Sisters of St. Joseph of Carondolet in their large convent next to the church, which was filled in the summer with sisters who were also attending USC.

Those were the days when the priest said Mass in Latin, mostly in silence, with his back to the people. Since I was the only male within the hallowed walls of the sacred convent, I did not have a little boy to serve the Mass. Instead, one of the sisters knelt at the communion rail, answered the responses in Latin, and rang the bell at the appointed times. Otherwise, I served myself since the sister was not allowed within the sanctuary during the Mass. (She was allowed, however, to enter the hallowed area after Mass in order to sweep and dust.) I was reminded of this situation recently while reminiscing with one of the sisters from those pre-Vatican II days with whom I attended USC, Sister Regina Clare Salazar, C.S.J. We laughed a little about it, but there was still a lingering pain because of the exclusion. After all, while I was saying Mass, the woman who was kneeling at the altar rail had been sanctified by the sacrament of baptism and further consecrated by the vows of religion, a daughter of God, a person who had dedicated her life to an important apostolate in the church, a bride of Christ and an imitator of the Virgin Mary, and yet she was excluded from the sanctuary where a small boy, had he been present, would have been allowed to minister. Strange is a very weak word for the thinking of that era which excluded her as well as other women. We should not judge the mentality which perpetrated such an indignity, but we must never return to it.

Now it is proper to see women, whether religious sisters or not, performing liturgical roles within the Mass: servers, lectors, acolytes, cantors, and ministers of hospitality and holy communion. I think of how the gospels assure us that women ministered to the needs of Jesus and his apostles. I find it particularly delightful when young girls serve at Mass. I remember how Jesus said, "Let the children [not just the boys] come to me." All of this is without prejudice to men and boys; reverse discrimination would be equally wrong. [One Sunday I observed to one of the lectors that we had no flowers on the altar. He pointed to the two girls, both about nine years of age, who would serve the Mass and said, "They are our flowers."]

St. Paul teaches us an important truth in his letter to the Galatians (3:27–28): "As many of you as were baptized into Christ have clothed yourselves with Christ..." Then he becomes very emphatic: "There is no longer Jew or Greek, there is no longer slave or free, there is no longer male and female; for all of you are one in Christ Jesus." I think back to my mother, to her two cousins who were Sisters of Mercy, to the Daughters of Charity who taught me in grade school, all of whom excelled in piety toward God and dedication to the church. And yet all suffered from an atmosphere of exclusion. I wish they could have lived to enjoy the Vatican II era in the church, even though there is much yet to be accomplished.

St. Vincent de Paul was very progressive in seventeenth-century France, especially in the manner in which he founded the Daughters of Charity. Once when I was distributing holy communion at St. Stephen's Church in New Orleans (where my brother, Clarence, is a very active parishioner), a Daughter of Charity stood next to me as a eucharistic minister. I thought that St. Vincent would say, "Yes, this is right. This is a good thing. I only wish that in my time I could have entrusted the Daughters of Charity with this beautiful ministry of love." Vincent, I believe, would say of St. Louise, his very close collaborator in ministry to the sick and the poor, that the hand which fed the poor, which washed the sores of the sick, which soothed those who were about to die, should also nourish God's people with the body and the blood of his beloved Son.

We have made progress in recognizing the dignity of women in the church, but that progress includes a better appreciation of men as well. This truth was brought home to me when in June of 1999 we observed the sixtieth anniversary of my brother's ordination as a priest. We arranged a well-deserved, although modest, celebration for Father Oscar at our old parish church, St. Joseph's in New Orleans. This was where he had celebrated his first solemn Mass on Trinity Sunday, June 4, 1939. One of the men at the sixtieth celebration had served Father Oscar's first solemn Mass at St. Joseph's back in 1939, and he insisted on serving his anniversary Mass. Of course he was now in his seventies. After the Mass, in a reflective mood which this type of observance often elicits, he remembered how, when he was serving the Mass in 1939, he looked up at Father Oscar's chalice on the altar. He told me that the chalice looked so beautiful that he wanted to reach out and touch it, but of course he knew that he could not. (At the time it was strictly forbidden for anyone other than a priest to touch the sacred vessels.) Then he said, with a twinkle in his eye, "But now I am a eucharistic minister."

From being forbidden even to touch a sacred vessel, he now distributes to others the very source of sacredness, Christ himself. I think that in honesty we must admit that before

Vatican II we were a little mixed up in our efforts to promote reverence. We gave indications that material things, even though they had been made of gold, were more precious than people, even though the people had been consecrated by the sacrament of baptism.

I think we can get a proper perspective by letting our thinking be influenced by an important aspect of Christmas. The eternal Son of God, in obedience to his Father, became incarnate in the womb of Mary and was born into our world, human like us in all things but sin. The Second Vatican Council, reflecting on the significance of this marvelous event, wrote: "By his incarnation and birth the Son of God has united himself with every human person. He worked with human hands, he thought with a human mind, he acted by human choice, and he loved with a human heart. Born of the Virgin Mary, he has become one of us, like us in all things but sin. He has shown us the way and if we follow it, life and death are made holy and take on a whole new meaning" (*The Pastoral Constitution on the Church in the Modern World*, 22).

In a sense it was not enough for God the Father to give our humanity a noble dignity by his almighty act of creation. He sent his Son to live our human life in order to raise us to an even higher dignity, a dignity which is conferred on us in the sacrament of baptism. The vessels used at Mass are blessed for their special purpose, but we have been consecrated by the sacrament of baptism. God has made us a chosen race, a royal priesthood, a holy nation, [his] own people (see 1 Pet 2:9–10). When we see lay people acting as ministers of the Mass, we ought to recognize that they are exercising their royal priesthood. That action tells us that they, and all of us, are more precious and deserving of much more reverence than the vessel which holds the consecrated hosts, the body of Christ, or the chalice which contains the blood of Christ. The Second Vatican Council has led us to recover many beautiful truths, not the least of which is the truth that people are more sacred than things.

Reflection and Discussion

- Think about ways in which you can show respect for the dignity of others, particularly for someone you dislike.

- Do we show enough respect and reverence for each other in church?

- Do you have an experience that illustrates the mistake of making things more sacred than people?

– 11 –

WHAT DOES CATHOLIC MEAN?

"...I truly understand that God shows no partiality, but in every nation anyone who fears him and does what is right is acceptable to him...." (Acts 10:34–35)

Let's go back to the year 1944. We are making a movie about Catholics. We call it *Going My Way*. The star is Bing Crosby who plays the part of a young priest whose name is Father O'Malley. The role of his pastor is given to Barry Fitzgerald who, if he were any more Irish, would not be able "to-talk-a-tall." In the rectory is a prominent picture of Pope Pius XII, who was born Eugenio Pacelli. That was the image of the church in the United States: Irish immigrants and their offspring who paid allegiance to an Italian pope. Even though the Irish were not the only Catholics, they had, for various reasons, risen to such an ascendancy, especially in the episcopacy, that they put their imprint on the American Catholic Church.

Let's move to 1994, only fifty years later. The young priest could be named Martinez or Nguyen or Kim or Ikeocha. His pastor might be Msgr. Moretti or Msgr. Chang or Msgr. Lapid. The picture on the wall is that of Karol Wojtyla, John Paul II, the first Polish pope. The image of the church in the United States had changed to include a large number of ethnic and cultural expressions, to be what the church had to struggle to become from the day of Pentecost—more Catholic.

After Jesus ascended into heaven, his disciples were alone and confused. They were not sure what they should do or even what it meant to be a disciple of Jesus. Some wondered whether they were another Jewish sect such as the Pharisees or the Zealots or the Essenes. They needed the Holy Spirit to enlighten them. On the day of Pentecost the apostles remembered Jesus' parting words to them: "You will receive power when the Holy Spirit has come upon you; and you will be my witnesses in Jerusalem, in all Judea and Samaria, and to the ends of the earth" (Acts 1:8). Things became clearer. They were to move beyond Jerusalem and Judea and Samaria to Gentile territory. The realization that Gentiles were called as well as Jews made them understand that Jesus had done something new. Antioch in Gentile Syria beyond the boundaries of Judea and Israel became the center for a large number of disciples, and it was in Antioch that the disciples were called Christians for the first time (Acts 11:26).

Only after much discussion, debate, and at times very heated arguments did the Christians come to see that Jesus had founded a church for all people of all times and all places. Then St. Ignatius, the bishop of Antioch, around the year A.D. 100, used the term *Catholic* for the first time to refer to his Christian community. The word, of course, means *universal*. It is a most appropriate word to characterize the church of Jesus Christ, and the name eventually became permanent and official. We now express our belief in the "one, holy, catholic, and apostolic church."

The church is not Italian or Irish or Polish. It is not Mexican or American or Canadian. It is universal. The Second Vatican Council was a striking witness to the catholicity of the church. When the First Vatican Council met in 1869 there were bishops from all over the world, but they were not indigenous bishops. For the most part they were European. Those who came from the United States were mostly Irish, with a few Germans. At Vatican

II the bishops were not only *from* all the countries of the world, they were *of* all the countries in the world. They were truly representative of the people whom they served.

After the *Constitution on the Sacred Liturgy* was published on December 4, 1963, it soon became obvious that the goals which the Constitution nobly expressed could be achieved only by a return to the vernacular in liturgical celebrations. I say "return" because the original practice was to celebrate the liturgy in the language of the people. In fact, the reason that Latin became a liturgical language in the first place was due to the principle that the language of the liturgy should be the language of the people. In Rome, until the third century, the liturgy was celebrated in Greek. Pope Victor I, who was African, may have started a movement to employ Latin, but it was probably Pope Callistus, a simple man who had at one time been a slave, who first insisted that Greek, despite its elegance and rich vocabulary, should be replaced by Latin since Latin had become the vernacular, the language of the people. Under the influence of Rome, Latin became widespread but it was never at any time the liturgical language of the universal church. The Eastern churches, in union with the pope, all employed their own languages up to and beyond the Second Vatican Council, not only in the countries of their origins but even in the United States.

Pope John Paul II gives excellent witness to the importance of the vernacular since he celebrates Mass in the language of the people wherever he goes, sometimes spending many hours in preparation with tutors in languages with which he is not familiar. It is reported that he had the most difficulty with Korean, but he insisted on mastering enough of that language to celebrate Mass for the people of Korea in their own language. The pope recognizes that there can be no substitute for the language which we learned as children from our parents.

When the liturgy employs the multiple languages of God's people, the experience of Pentecost is repeated. On the first

Pentecost, even though the people were from diverse regions throughout the Near East, they all heard the apostles speaking in their own tongue about the marvels God had accomplished in his Son. The importance, then, of every vernacular must be insisted upon. That God is worshipped in the multiple languages of his diverse children reflects the catholicity of our faith. Pope John Paul II declared in his book, *Crossing the Threshold of Hope,* that the Second Vatican Council was like a new Pentecost for the church. In celebrating the liturgical observance of Pentecost we give thanks and praise to God for calling us into the church, which is one, holy, catholic, and apostolic.

The change from Latin with its European roots to the vernaculars of the world was more than a way of facilitating full, active participation in the liturgy; it was an expression of a deeper understanding of the church as Catholic. Latin, or any single language, is not the means for oneness in the church. Sharing in the Word of God and the same holy Eucharist are the means for the church to be both one and holy. Actually Latin is well honored in her daughter languages, especially Italian, Spanish, and Portuguese, that have softened her pronunciation, simplified her grammar, and enriched her vocabulary. Not just these Romance languages, but all the many vernaculars of the liturgy manifest that the church has been true to its mission to make disciples of all the nations, and these languages are a sign that the church is now truly catholic, or universal.

The church was multilingual from the beginning. As the church was born from the pierced side of Christ when he hung upon the cross, above his head was the inscription, "Jesus of Nazareth, the King of the Jews" (John 19:19). It was written in Hebrew, Latin, and Greek, which were the languages, in addition to Aramaic, spoken in Palestine. Some scholars are of the opinion that Jesus knew something of all of these languages, but his vernacular was Aramaic. The Old Testament was composed in Hebrew, except for the deutero-canonical books, which were in Greek. Some say that the original of St. Matthew's Gospel was Hebrew, but a better opinion seems to be that it was Aramaic, which was almost immediately translated into Greek. Greek is the language of the New Testament. Some Aramaic expressions were preserved within the Greek original, the most important of which is *Abba,* Jesus' word for his Father. In the third century Latin became the language of the church in Rome, and for the most part that of the missionaries who spread the faith from Europe.

These languages are part of our heritage which should be reflected in our liturgy. We need to remember that some familiar words which are part of the Mass are Hebrew, not only *Amen,* the universal liturgical word, but *Alleluia* and *Hosanna.* On occasion it would be well to substitute the Greek *Kyrie eleison, Christe eleison, Kyrie eleison* for Lord have mercy, Christ have mercy, Lord have mercy. A simply sung *Agnus Dei* for Lamb of God can be the Latin part of the Mass. All we need in addition is Aramaic, especially Jesus' own precious title for God, *Abba.* Do you think we could ever become comfortable in praying "Abba in heaven, hallowed be your name"? Some people are offended by the use of "Father" for God since they construe it as masculine. They substitute "Good and gracious God" or "God our Creator," both of which fail to convey Jesus' revelation that God's relationship with us is that of parent to child. Maybe *Abba* is the answer.

William Shakespeare wrote that he knew a little Latin and less Greek. Because of our heritage every Catholic ought to know enough to pray a few words, not only in Latin and Greek, but in Hebrew and Aramaic. And yet, nothing can substitute for our vernacular, whatever it may be, since our mother tongue, the language of the heart, is the primary expression of our culture.

From the very beginning, as we have seen, the church has struggled to be truly universal. One problem in our era is a failure to make a distinction between unity and uniformity. It is an easy mistake to believe that uniformity is necessary for unity, that Catholics in their worship should all use the same language and follow the same practices so that the Mass would look and sound the same everywhere in the world. The fact is that the Eastern Rite churches without Latin or any single language, and despite many various ritual traditions, have maintained Catholic unity, whereas Archbishop LeFevre, who insisted on the retention of Latin and the "Tridentine" ritual, broke with the Holy See and became schismatic.

The Second Vatican Council in its *Constitution on the Sacred Liturgy* (37 and 38) moved to correct the error of equating unity with uniformity by declaring: "Even in the liturgy the Church has no wish to impose a rigid uniformity in matters which do not involve the faith or the good of the whole community. Rather she respects and fosters the spiritual adornments and gifts of the various races and people. Provided that the substantial unity of the Roman rite is maintained, the revision of liturgical books should allow for legitimate variations and adaptation to different groups, regions, and peoples, especially in mission lands. Where opportune, the same rule applies to the structuring of rites and the devising of rubrics." In this declaration from the Constitution, may I add emphasis to the word *substantial* in the phrase "provided that the *substantial* unity of the Roman rite is maintained..."? In other words, at least minor details are to admit of adaptations.

It has remained difficult to achieve adaptations in accord with cultural differences. In fact, when my confrere, Archbishop Annibale Bugnini, C.M., one of the chief architects of "Vatican II liturgy," attempted to formulate a concrete plan for cultural adaptations, he was "kicked upstairs" (or downstairs, depending on how you look at it). After having dedicated some forty years of his priestly life to the sacred liturgy, he was removed from his position as Secretary of the Congregation for Divine Worship and was made Pro-Nuncio to Iran (!) where he died in 1982.

In order to be open to the catholicity of the church, we must recognize that our culture conditions all of us and disposes us to embrace certain values. Some people criticize Padre Junipero Serra, the apostle of California, for trying to turn the Indians into Spaniards. Of course he did. How could he have been expected to have done anything else? His cultural conditioning led him to believe that to be Catholic was to be Spanish, just as in a later generation the Irish clergy thought that to be Catholic was to be Irish. Hilaire Belloc, the English Catholic who was born in France, wrote in 1920 that "The Faith is Europe and Europe is the Faith." We cannot judge, let alone condemn, people of another era for their cultural conditioning, but after Vatican Council II the limitations of such conditioning can no longer be accepted.

As happens with everyone, I was conditioned by the religious culture in which I grew up. That was in New Orleans, Louisiana during the 1930s. New Orleans, especially at that time, was a very Catholic city. In fact, in our neighborhood there was only one family which was not Catholic. We kids persecuted their little girl. We called her the "Protestant brat." (I drop my head in shame as I think about that now.) My father, however, had some business associates who were not Catholic and when the wife of one of them died, I was dragged by my parents to her wake service in the funeral parlor, as we called mortuaries in those days. The room was hushed and in the back someone was playing softly on a small organ. I followed my parents to the front where some object seemed to be the center of attention. It was the casket. My parents stopped and looked at the deceased. As I stood on tiptoe to try to see, I heard my mother whisper to my father, "Doesn't she look nice!" Then we went and sat in what resembled a pew. Passive silence reigned. I thought I was in church.

In contrast was my experience when Cardinal Eugenio Pacelli was elected pope in 1939 (I was just nine years old). No one owned a TV in those days (TV was just being introduced at the New York World's Fair), but we did have Pathé News in the movie theater. I remember vividly seeing the new pope being carried on the *sedia gestatoria* into St. Peter's Basilica. The people were going wild—clapping, yelling, and chanting "Viva il papa!" And I thought, "In church?" I was shocked because during elementary school I used to get in trouble with the nuns at Mass for merely looking across the aisle at the girls. What was scandalous to me because of my Jansenistic atmosphere was perfectly normal, even devout, for the Italians. Culture is not the same as religion.

One Sunday at St. Julie's Church in Newbury Park, California the newly formed choir remained in the front of the church after Mass, receiving the congratulations of some of the assembly. I was in the rear, greeting the people as they were leaving, when one of them stopped and insisted, "Father, you go up there and tell those people that Catholics do not talk in church!" As pleasantly as possible I explained to her that I could not do so because I was convinced that God the Father was delighted, just as any parent would be, to see his children exchanging pleasantries in his home.

I have found that one of the most controversial aspects of culture revolves around the matter of reverence. These days some people complain that there is no reverence in church, by which they mean that the Mass is no longer overlaid with a heavy silence as in the so-called Tridentine Mass. One could answer by pointing out that reverence is in the heart and the mind of the believer, but the truth is that liturgy by its nature demands that there be external signs of internal sentiments. The liturgy is composed of body as well as soul. External signs of internal reverence are important, regardless of one's culture.

The first sign of reverence is that shortly after we have assembled for Mass, the priest invites us to acknowledge our sinfulness. A moment of silence follows. This simple act manifests our unworthiness before the infinite holiness of God. It is an act of reverence. During the liturgy of the word we honor Christ present in the holy scriptures. The inspired word is proclaimed from a large book, usually red in color, which by its size and beauty manifests the reverence we owe to Christ present in his word. To this proclamation of the word in the readings we respond by saying "Thanks be to God," and to proclamation in the gospel we respond by saying "Praise to you, Lord Jesus Christ." Thanks and praise are sentiments due to Christ in his divinity; they express our reverence.

In the low Mass before the restoration mandated by the Second Vatican Council, only the priest prayed the *Sanctus,* and that silently. Now we all sing or say in response to God's magnificence, "Holy, holy, holy Lord, God of power and might!" The triple "holy" is a form of the superlative degree and expresses our profound adoration of the majesty of God. When we proclaim the mystery of our faith, "Christ has died, Christ is risen, Christ will come again," our hearts should be filled with awe and wonder at the incomprehensible love of Christ for us. With reverence we acknowledge that Christ, by his death and resurrection, is the Savior of the world.

Our faith teaches us that Christ is present not only in the inspired word and in the holy Eucharist, but also in his people, who form his mystical body. The sign of peace is a recognition of the presence of Christ in others and a sign of reverence. During the sign of peace we need to remember the words of Jesus, "Just as you did it to one of the least of these who are members of my family, you did it to me" (Matt 25:40). In coming to communion we are asked to show a sign of reverence by bowing to the presence of Christ before we receive the body of the Lord and before we drink from the cup. A particularly beautiful sign of reverence is when we form our hands into a throne to receive Christ the King.

We may tend to equate reverence with soberness, and to mistake mood for substance. Perhaps we yearn for an atmosphere of quiet and reflection. Such we need and must find for ourselves outside the liturgy. Private devotion is indispensable, but the liturgy is not meant to fulfill that need. Liturgy is the celebration of God's family. True reverence is a form of respect which we pay to each other at Mass. The word *respect* comes from the Latin which means "to look again." When we give liturgy a second look, when we respect it for what it truly is, we recognize that it is meant to take place within the atmosphere of a happy family, the family of God. When we discard the cultural caricature of reverence as solemn and somber rather than as joyful and jubilant, active participation will allow us to experience the profound reverence of Vatican II liturgy.

Not all cultural expressions are acceptable. The *Constitution on the Sacred Liturgy* (37) warns against practices which are "indissolubly bound up with superstition and error." Even practices that, although not superstitious or erroneous, interfere with the proper celebration of liturgy are not to influence our worship. Whatever adaptations for language and culture may be made, the basic principles of Vatican II's *Constitution on the Sacred Liturgy* must be followed. Among the most important of those principles, I suggest, are the following:

> "Every liturgical celebration, because it is an action of Christ the priest and of his body, the Church, is a sacred action surpassing all others. No other action of the Church can match its claim to efficacy nor equal the degree of it" (7). There is to be no debate about the importance of the liturgy. To the liturgy all must come with faith that Christ is present and active in four ways: in his people gathered in his name, in the priest presiding in his person, in his word proclaimed, and in his Eucharist celebrated. Neglecting or minimizing any of these actions of Christ is unacceptable.

Because of the importance of the liturgy "Mother Church earnestly desires that all the faithful be led to that full, conscious, and active participation in the liturgical celebration which is demanded by the very nature of the liturgy. Such participation…is their right and duty by reason of their baptism. In the restoration and promotion of the sacred liturgy, this full and active participation by all the people is the aim to be considered before all else, for it is the primary and indispensable source from which the faithful are to derive the true Christian spirit" (14).

A passive, "quiet" liturgy is not in accord with the principles of the Constitution. The Constitution clarifies the nature of active participation: "The people are to be encouraged to take part by means of acclamations, responses, psalmody, antiphons, and songs, as well as by actions, gestures, and bodily attitudes. And at the proper times all should observe a reverent silence" (30). Further, "In liturgical celebrations, all persons should perform their role by doing solely but totally what the nature of things and liturgical norms require of them" (28). Finally, everyone must remember this declaration of the Constitution: "Zeal for the promotion and restoration of the liturgy is rightly held to be a sign of the providential disposition of God in our time, as a movement of the Holy Spirit in his Church. It is today a distinguishing mark of the Church's life, indeed of the whole tenor of contemporary religious thought and action." (43)

Paradoxically the church, to be fully Catholic, must be freed from a single culture in order to embrace all cultures. Vatican II's *Constitution on the Church in the Modern World* declared that "the Church, sent to all peoples of every time and place, is not bound exclusively and indissolubly to any race or nation, nor to any particular way of life or any customary pattern of living, ancient or recent. Faithful to her own tradition and at the same time conscious of her universal mission, she can enter into communion with various cultural modes, to her own enrichment and theirs too" (58).

The church by embracing all cultures shows forth her beauty and her true character as the Catholic Church.

Reflection and Discussion

- Think of some ways in which our cultural practices or outlooks are distinct from religion.

- How important is the vernacular to you?

- Reflect on the statement: "Paradoxically the Church to be fully Catholic must be freed from a single culture in order to embrace all cultures."

– 1 2 –

PENANCE:
A CELEBRATION

"Son, your sins are forgiven." (Mark 2:5)

In a previous generation confession was pretty usual among some Catholics. When I was growing up in parochial school we kids were paraded over to church before every First Friday for confessions, and not a few adults had the practice of going to confession every Saturday. We had a sincere desire to humble ourselves before the mercy of God, but there were other reasons, truth to tell, for frequent confession. We were given the impression that it was rather easy to commit a mortal sin since almost all transgressions were considered to be grave. We developed an image of God from what we heard preached in the pulpit and taught in the classroom which made God to be a not-very-jovial version of the Santa Claus who was "keeping a list and checking it twice" and who would find out "who had been naughty and nice." We were also unaware that the Eucharist is a sacrament of forgiveness and reconciliation. The Eucharist, of course, is not a substitute for penance but it is the solid teaching of the church that one effect of a devout holy communion is forgiveness of venial sins.

Although during my youth confession was a frequent experience, we would never have thought of it as a celebration. Now, whenever we go to confession and for whatever reasons, we ought to give careful consideration to *celebrating* the sacrament of penance. The first meaning of liturgical celebration is that it is a gathering of people. During Advent and Lent very many parishes in the United States offer the opportunity to participate in what we call a penance service (the technical term is "Rite II of the Sacrament of Penance"). We come together to hear the Word of God, to acknowledge our sinfulness, to pray for each other, to confess our sins to a priest, to receive absolution, and to fulfill our penance. Participating in the sacrament together is the Catholic way to do things. It is a celebration.

The second meaning of liturgical celebration is that we offer thanks and praise to God. We acknowledge that our God is a God of compassion and mercy, that he is eager to forgive our sins and to welcome us into his warm embrace. We express our praise not only in the prayers we say but even by the very fact that we take part in the penance service and confess our sins with the confidence that they will be forgiven. We would not come to the service if we did not believe that God is compassionate and we certainly would not confess our sins if we were not convinced that God is merciful. During the penance service we give thanks and praise to God for his compassion and mercy. *That* is a celebration.

The third meaning of celebration is that we express our love and concern for each other. We pray that we may all benefit from the beautiful sacrament of penance, that we may experience the healing balm of God's mercy, and that in our daily lives our love for God and each other may grow stronger and more faithful. That kind of prayer is a celebration.

We ought to remember as Catholics that we may go to confession as frequently as we experience the need or the desire, provided we do not act out of scrupulosity or a failure to value the holy Eucharist as a sacrament of reconciliation. In fact, we should not ordinarily wait until Advent or Lent to go to confession because we can benefit from the sacrament by a frequency that is more than once or twice a year. Nevertheless, when our parish offers a penance service we ought to make every effort to participate in this important celebration.

My experience tells me that Catholics need to be more aware that the primary purpose of the sacrament of penance is liturgical, and is intended to give praise to God. At Mass the priest introduces the eucharistic prayer with the invitation: "Let us give thanks to the Lord, our God." In our response we agree that it is right to give our thanks and praise. Then in many forms of the preface, the priest goes on to say, "Father, we do well always and everywhere to give you thanks." One of the "always" times is when we go to confession, and one of the "everywhere" places is the church, or any other location, during the celebration of the sacrament of penance.

At the conclusion of a penance service, the directive tells us that "it is fitting for all to sing a psalm or hymn or to say a litany in acknowledgment of God's power and mercy." That is an expression of thanks and praise to God which fulfills the primary purpose of liturgy. We do well to recognize that not only our words but also our actions proclaim the power and mercy of God. Think about going to a doctor whom you trust and respect. You place your illness in his hands, so to speak, to deal with as he knows best. If it is a matter of serious surgery, you are entrusting him not only with your health but with your life itself. All of your actions implicitly praise him for his knowledge and skill. When we come before the Lord in the sacrament of penance, we show our faith in his mercy and pardon. We ask him to heal us of the illness of sin. We need have no fears about the most serious of sins, those sins which threaten to destroy the gift of everlasting life, since we believe that we can trust to God the surgery which is needed to remove effectively and completely the cancer of even mortal sin.

In his Pastoral Letter, "In Praise of God's Mercy," Cardinal Roger Mahony of Los Angeles, in commenting on how we need to appreciate this sacrament, wrote: "Perhaps the greatest difficulty of all lies in accepting the truth that God is one whose mercy knows no bounds." Accepting this truth is difficult because we find it very hard to forgive those who have offended us deeply. We may say, "I forgive, but I just can't forget." Our forgiveness has its limit. We find that there is a "last straw which breaks the camel's back," and we naturally assume that God is as limited in his willingness to forgive as we are. Our limitations should help us to realize that total forgiveness is a divine attribute, such as is God's power to create or to annihilate. Actually God's mercy annihilates our sins. He never says "I just can't forget"; he creates anew within us our pristine holiness. Acknowledging how God forgives completely is an act of liturgy, a form of thanks and praise.

Go to confession. Celebrate the sacrament of penance. And remember that all your actions are "in praise of God's mercy."

Reflection and Discussion

- How can the sacrament of penance be considered a celebration—especially individual confession?

- How is the very act of "going to confession" a way of praising God?

- What are some of your difficulties in "going to confession"?

– 1 3 –

ALL SINS ARE SOCIAL

If one member suffers, all suffer together with it.... (1 Cor 12:26)

Confessing one's sins is a pretty personal matter, as personal as going to your doctor. When you are in the doctor's waiting room, you do not stand up and announce to everyone present why you are seeing him. When your turn comes to go into the examining room, you want to be alone with the doctor and you probably speak with him in hushed tones. You may even be a little embarrassed.

Sin can be embarrassing. Of course during the entrance rite of the Mass we acknowledge that we are all sinners. I think we have no hesitancy about that, but when it comes to specifics we usually value privacy. The church, as a matter of fact, has never required that people confess their specific sins publicly in order to receive absolution. The church, in accord with scripture, only asks that we acknowledge that we are sinners.

All of this does not mean that sin has nothing to do with others in the church. We are the body of Christ and our actions affect the members of the body for good or for ill. St. Paul comments: "No one ever hates his own body, but he nourishes and tenderly cares for it, just as Christ does for the church, because we are members of his body" (Eph 5:29–30). And yet at times, far from taking care of our bodies, we do things which are injurious, such as smoking, failing to exercise, or overindulging in food or drink. The whole body suffers from this abuse. Drugs make slaves of people and have far-reaching effects in their entire being, not just in an isolated part of their body. Sin is like that. No matter how hidden or individual we think a sin to be, it has an effect upon all the people of the church. "If one member suffers, all the members suffer with it." A secular ethic asserts that actions are acceptable as long as they do not harm another person, and that the actions of consenting adults fall outside the norm of morality. This fallacy rests upon a failure to understand the unity of the human race, and even more profoundly the nature of the church as the body of Christ.

The truth is that there are no victimless crimes nor are there any sins which do not injure the body of Christ. Just as harm is done to the whole church by sin, so reconciliation must be with the whole church. This reconciliation comes through the bishop or priest who stands in the person of the entire church.

Sometimes people ask, "Why do I have to go to confession? Can't God forgive my sins directly if I am truly sorry?" This question reveals a failure to understand not only the sacrament of penance, but the nature of sin. When we come to church for confession, we are not to go to a microphone and announce our sins to all present and ask their forgiveness; however, for a fruitful celebration of the sacrament of penance we do have to understand the social consequences of sin and the need for reconciliation with the whole church.

When people protest, "Can't God forgive my sins without my going to confession?" I usually respond by admitting that God can, of course, forgive sins in any manner he chooses, but as a matter of fact he has provided a sacrament for that purpose. It may also be said, as we have just seen, that all sins are social, that they injure the entire church, and so reconciliation must be not only with God but with the church.

There is still another way of looking at the matter. If we could pose to Catholics of the early centuries the question about why we have to confess sins to a priest, they would be befuddled by it. They would protest that they do not understand the problem and would ask us, "What are you talking about?" Pristine Catholics recognized that the church is God's chosen means for contact with us. They gave no thought to seeking forgiveness from God on their own without relying on the church. There was simply no idea of going outside the church in order to get to God. The church is itself a sacrament, the way in which God has chosen to communicate with us. The seven sacraments, including penance, are specific expressions of the one sacrament, the church.

The Second Vatican Council recaptured this pristine understanding of the church and taught that "the Church is the universal sacrament of salvation, simultaneously manifesting and exercising the mystery of God's love for his people" (*The Pastoral Constitution on the Church in the Modern World*, 45). Forgiveness of sins and reconciliation with God come in and through the church. If there has been a falling off in the use of the sacrament of penance in our time, one reason is a failure to understand the nature of the church. This fact is ironic in light of the fact that Vatican II was a Council by the church and about the church. Many obstacles, however, have prevented us from absorbing its message, such as individualism in personal piety, a shallow approach to devotion, a failure or unwillingness to grow beyond a child's level of faith and understanding, a false ecumenism which suggests that one religion is really the same as another, and even in some cases an intransigent objection to the Second Vatican Council in general.

The renewal of the sacrament of penance depends on a renewal of what it means to be a Catholic. We will make progress in understanding the sacrament when we realize that "it has pleased God to save us and make us holy, not merely as individuals without any mutual bonds, but by forming us into a single people" (*Dogmatic Constitution on the Church*, 9), when we understand that prayer in the first instance means liturgical prayer in community, and when we see that devotion to the Blessed Sacrament is essentially expressed through the celebration of the Mass as God's family. No sacrament, including penance, will be understood without understanding the church as the universal sacrament. The profound truth of faith is that reconciliation ultimately is not with God and the church, but with God *through* the church. Thinking and acting as Catholics positively and profoundly influences all aspects of our faith, including the sacrament of penance.

When we go to confession, we receive absolution. That is a great blessing. And yet St. Paul reminds us of the words of the Lord Jesus: "It is more blessed to give than to receive" (Acts 20:35). In the confessing of our sins the two actions of giving and receiving are not separated. Perhaps we can see just why this is true by remembering that "confession" is the celebration of the sacrament of penance. All seven sacraments are part of the liturgy, and all liturgy is worship; it is giving thanks and praise to God.

Reflection and Discussion

- Read St. Mark's Gospel, chapter 2, verses 1 to 12. Describe the aspects of the sacrament of penance that you see in this passage.

- Read chapter 12 of St. Paul's Letter to the Romans. How does this chapter have an application to the sacrament of penance?

- Some Catholics complain about bad experiences with the sacrament of penance. What have been some of your positive experiences?

– 1 4 –

MOTHER, DISCIPLE,
AND MODEL

"Here am I, the servant of the Lord...." (Luke 1:38)

Every Catholic knows that Mary is an important part of our lives because she was an important part of God's plan for our salvation. The Fathers of the Second Vatican Council had no intention of ignoring Mary. That was unthinkable. But they did have to decide whether they should produce a separate document on Mary or whether they should include Mary in the *Dogmatic Constitution on the Church (Lumen Gentium)*. The debate was long and at times heated. The vote by a narrow margin favored including Mary in the document on the church so that the eighth chapter of that document is entitled "The Role of the Blessed Virgin Mary, Mother of God, in the Mystery of Christ and the Church." This chapter acknowledges Mary as "the supereminent and uniquely special member of the Church as well as its model in faith and love and its most outstanding exemplar" (53).

In accord with her prophecy in the *Magnificat*, "All generations will call me blessed," Catholic piety has developed a deep devotion to Mary. Many Catholics love to pray the rosary, others have a favorite novena, and still others follow the church's prayer book, the Liturgy of the Hours. Essential though prayer is, devotion includes more. We say that imitation is the highest form of flattery. Imitation is also the highest form of devotion. The gospels present us with five specific instances in which we can see Mary as a model for disciples of her Son so that our devotion may become imitation.

We first encounter Mary when the angel Gabriel announced to her that she was to be the Mother of Jesus, the Son of God. Mary was but a young girl. She was troubled by this angelic appearance and confounded by his message. She realized that she did not understand all that was involved. Despite her fears she said, "Here am I, the servant of the Lord; let it be with me according to your word" (Luke 1:38). She embraced God's will. She put herself into God's hands as his servant girl so that God's plan could be accomplished through her. In that moment the eternal Word became flesh. Mary's life was completely changed. Like any mother, she was no longer an individual. She carried another person in her womb. If Mary were our contemporary, she would go to a doctor who would confirm her pregnancy. He would then warn her, "Young lady, you are now responsible for another life. This is a serious obligation. It means no smoking, no drinking, a healthy diet, and proper exercise. Take care of this life within you." Even without a modern doctor's instructions, Mary knew what she had to do for Jesus. She had to cherish, protect, and nourish the life of Jesus within her. Mary's devotion to the will of God and its consequences is Mary's first example for us.

The second example was occasioned by Gabriel's informing Mary that Elizabeth, her kinswoman, had conceived a child in her old age. The angel told Mary about Elizabeth to assure her that nothing is impossible with God, not even conception by a virgin, but Mary heard his words as a call to action. She thought, "Elizabeth needs me." St. Luke in his Gospel tells us that Mary went in haste to be with Elizabeth. It was, of course, a journey on foot. I imagine that Mary had to get permission from Joseph to go since they were already espoused, and she probably had to talk one or more of her girlfriends into accompanying her since it was unheard of that a young girl would travel alone. All the inconvenience notwithstanding, Mary was eager to make the journey. After she arrived, I presume Mary tended to the household chores. She did the cooking, washing, and cleaning, and every day she went to the well to get water. She made sure that Elizabeth was comfortable. Mary was a person of action.

When Elizabeth saw Mary coming to her she was overwhelmed, not only because she was moved by the generosity of her young kinswoman, but because she had received a revelation that Mary was carrying in her womb their Lord and Savior. That is why Elizabeth cried out, "Why has this happened to me, that the mother of my Lord comes to me?" (Luke 1:43). Mary immediately deflected the praise from herself and directed it to God. She said, "My soul magnifies the Lord, and my spirit rejoices in God my Savior, for he has looked with favor on the lowliness of his servant" (Luke 1:46–48). In her humility Mary recognized that it was right and just to give thanks and praise to God. She is a model for worship.

Mary's worship of God the Father reached its highest expression at the foot of the cross. St. John tells us in his Gospel: "Standing near the cross of Jesus were his mother, and his mother's sister, Mary the wife of Clopas, and Mary Magdalene." And the disciple [whom Jesus loved] was standing beside [his mother]. In reflecting on this event, Pope Pius XII, in 1943, wrote these beautiful words: "Mary, always most intimately united with her son, offered him on Calvary to the Eternal Father for all the children of Adam sin-stained by his fall, and her mother's rights and her mother's love were included in the holocaust" (Encyclical on *The Church as the Mystical Body of Christ* [*Mystici Corporis Christi*], 127). This was Mary's eucharistic sacrifice. The little band of three women and the beloved disciple, standing with her at the cross, followed her example of worship. Mary is a model for offering the eucharistic sacrifice.

Mary was a contemplative. This truth was the foundation of her piety and her dedication. St. Luke says that, following the birth of Jesus which was hailed by the angels and greeted by the shepherds, "Mary treasured all these words and pondered them in her heart" (Luke 2:19). After Jesus had been found in the temple, after being missing for three days, St. Luke says, "His mother treasured all these things in her heart" (2:51). We can be sure that this contemplative spirit which began with the birth of Jesus carried Mary through her entire life, even to the mysterious moment of the death of her Son by crucifixion. Because Mary had lived a life of contemplation, she could accept God's will for the sacrificial death of her Son. It was her ultimate act of conformity to God's will. Mary was a reflective person, a contemplative.

Mary is our model in these five ways: she dedicated herself to God's will; she was a person of charitable action; she gave thanks and praise to God; she joined Jesus in the offering of the sacrifice of the cross; and she was a contemplative. Mary is indeed, as the Second Vatican Council teaches, "the supereminent and uniquely special member of the Church as well as its model in faith and love and its most outstanding exemplar" (*Dogmatic Constitution on the Church*, 53). Where do we begin to imitate this extraordinary woman? I suggest that we begin with contemplation. We must not be afraid of that word as if it suggests some ethereal experiences of cloistered monks and nuns, far above our simple, ordinary lives. Reflection should be characteristic of every intelligent person, and it must be the foundation of our lives as disciples of Jesus. The busier our lives, the more we must take time to reflect on the meaning of our existence, to determine where we are going, to decide how we are to handle the challenges of our lives, and above all to discern how we can see God at work in everything we do and in everything we experience. In particular we must be attentive to the scriptures as we hear them proclaimed in the liturgy and as we read them privately. Like Mary we must treasure all these things in memory and reflect on them in our hearts. When we are contemplatives we are then open to God's grace so that the Holy Spirit may direct us to that example of Mary which we are invited to follow during a particular moment of our lives. This contemplation depends on a profound faith which moves us to see that the only way to make sense of life is to embrace God's will. Conformity to God's will does not make life easy but it does give it meaning, especially when in accord with God's will we are people of the sacraments. Through the sacraments of initiation, baptism, confirmation, and first Eucharist, Jesus comes alive within us as members of his Mystical Body. We realize how much we must nourish that life by word and sacrament and protect it from the dangers of sin. We perceive that Christian mortification is not a form of hatred for ourselves but of protection for the life of Jesus within us.

Through a dedication to God's will we grasp that God does not want us to live isolated lives without any concern for others, but that like Mary we are to be people of action which manifests our love for each other. Through the liturgical scriptures we understand that whatever we do to even the least of Christ's brothers and sisters we do to him. Through devotion to Mary we also discover that in reaching out to others we are bringing Christ to them as Mary brought Christ to Elizabeth and her baby. Our devotion begins to be based on the truth that our lives are about loving Christ, a reality expressed by St. Augustine.

We are so blessed in our faith and our many other gifts from God that the church in her prayer book, The Liturgy of the Hours, directs us to offer Mary's prayer, the *Magnificat,* at evening prayer every day of the year without exception. Joining Mary and all those who through contemplation recognize God as the source of our every blessing, we say, "My soul proclaims the greatness of the Lord and my spirit finds joy in God, my Savior" (from *Evening Prayer*). This beautiful prayer of thanks and praise leads us to the greatest act of thanks and praise, which is the celebration of the holy Eucharist.

During the celebration of the Eucharist our model is Mary who stood at the foot of the cross. We now take the place of those who accompanied her at the cross—her sister, Mary the wife of Clopas, Mary Magdalene, and the beloved disciple. We are not deprived from participating in the greatest act of worship ever offered on this earth simply because we were born many centuries after the event. The Eucharist is the sacrament of the death and resurrection of Jesus. It is the living memorial of the paschal mystery, the mystery of faith. Looking up to our Father in heaven, we say "We thank you for counting us worthy to stand in your presence and serve you." The celebration of the Eucharist leads us back to our starting point, to where we begin our imitation of Mary by being people of contemplation. The celebration of the Eucharist must be the mainstay of our reflection. The Second Vatican Council, in its document on priestly ministry, declares that "the eucharistic action is the very heartbeat of the congregation of the faithful over which the priest presides," and it instructs priests that they are to move the people "to offer to God the Father the divine Victim in the sacrifice of the Mass and to join to it the offering of their own lives" (*Decree on the Ministry and Life of Priests,* 5). People and priests at Mass have no better model than Mary.

The Fathers of the Second Vatican Council were moved by the Holy Spirit to include Mary in their *Constitution on the Church.* They recalled that as the newly born church awaited the coming of the Holy Spirit at Pentecost, "[the apostles] were constantly devoting themselves to prayer, together with certain women, including Mary the mother of Jesus..." (Acts 1:14).

In the *Dogmatic Constitution on the Church,* the Fathers of the Second Vatican Council have given us a beautiful portrait of Mary as mother, disciple, and model. This is their heartfelt wish for us: "Let the faithful remember that true devotion consists neither in fruitless and passing emotion, nor in a certain vain credulity; rather, it proceeds from true faith, by which we are led to know the excellence of the Mother of God and are moved to a filial love toward our mother and to the imitation of her virtues" (67).

Reflection and Discussion

- Discuss the ways in which you see Mary as the perfect disciple who was committed to God's will, eager to be active and helpful, humbly offering all the glory to God, sharing the great sacrifice of the cross, and dedicated to contemplation.

- How can you in your life imitate Mary as a disciple of the Lord?

- Think about your favorite images of Mary (statues or pictures) and what they mean to you.

– 15 –

LOAVES AND FISHES

"...the bread that I will give for the life of the world is my flesh."
(John 6:51)

Jesus worked many miracles during his time on earth. Everyone remembers that at the wedding at Cana in Galilee he changed water into wine. John alone tells that story, in his second chapter. One of my favorite miracles involves a funeral procession. A widow was about to bury her only son. Jesus was moved with pity. He said to the woman, "Do not weep." He raised the boy to life and gave him back to his mother. Only Luke tells that story, in his seventh chapter. One day when Jesus went to Peter's home, he found Peter's mother-in-law in bed with a fever. He immediately restored her to health. Mark (1:30) and Luke (4:38) tell that story, but not Matthew or John. Of all Jesus' many miracles only one has been recounted by each of the four gospels. That fact tells us that this miracle is very significant. It is the feeding of the five thousand with five loaves and two fish.

The story is essentially the same in all four gospels but each has its own specific contribution to the narrative. St. Mark was the first to write a gospel. One of his characteristics is that he loved to use details to paint graphic pictures, and graphic indeed is the scene on a spring day when Jesus had the people sit down "in groups on the green grass." St. Mark wrote that "they sat down in groups of hundreds and fifties." Their clothes, though they were poor, were of various colors and reflected the beauty of God's creation. St. Mark was not himself an eyewitness of this event, but some scholars believe that the description came to him from people who were there. It was an experience they would never have forgotten down to the smallest particulars. St. Mark's account is in chapter 6, verses 32–44.

St. Matthew is next to be considered (14:13–21). One of his contributions, together with that of St. Luke, was to note that Jesus' miracle was so generous that even after all had eaten, there were twelve baskets of bread left over! St. Matthew also lets us know that Jesus fed more than the five thousand men who were there. Women and children were present also, but for some reason no one bothered to count them! St. Matthew tells us that before Jesus fed the people, he cured their sick, but St. Mark chose to emphasize that when Jesus saw the people like sheep without a shepherd he began to teach them at great length. St. Luke included both facts: "Jesus spoke to them of the reign of God and he healed all who were in need of healing."

St. Mark, St. Matthew, and St. Luke all include the detail that Jesus shared his ministry. They noted that Jesus gave the loaves to his disciples to distribute. St. John added a distinctive note which is of particular interest to me. He tells us that Andrew said to Jesus, "There is a boy here who has five barley loaves and two fish." I have a very vivid memory of a stained glass window in the church of my youth, St. Joseph's in New Orleans, which depicts that young boy looking up to Jesus and offering him his basket with the loaves and the fish. I used to stare at the window and wish that I could have been that boy. Many years later I returned as a priest to St. Joseph's and I immediately went in search of the window. No such window exists, at least not in St. Joseph's Church. Where, I asked myself, did my vivid memory come from? I have no answer to that question.

One of St. John's distinctive notes is his observation that the Jewish feast of Passover was near. That tells us that it was springtime, but more important, this detail suggests to us that Jesus was thinking of the Christian Passover, the paschal mystery of his death and resurrection. And so St. John alone follows the story of the feeding of the five thousand by his presentation of a sermon Jesus preached the following day in the synagogue of Capernaum in which he called for faith in himself and faith in his promise of the Eucharist.

Actually all four evangelists composed their story in such a way that we readily think of the Eucharist. It was their way of saying that everything Jesus said and did led up to his death and resurrection, which we celebrate in the Mass; the Eucharist is the sacrament of Jesus' death and resurrection, his paschal mystery.

Notice the parallels of the Mass with the gospels. When the assembly gathers, they resemble the people who sat in groups on the grass to eat the loaves and fish. During the opening rite of the Mass Jesus sees us gathered as the sheep of his flock, and he heals us when we express sorrow for our sins during the penitential rite. Then he teaches us in the liturgy of the word. He speaks to us of the reign of God. Those who bring up the bread and wine during the preparation of the gifts are replacing that lad who offered the five loaves and the two fish to Jesus. Jesus "took the five loaves and the two fish and raising his eyes to heaven pronounced a blessing over them, broke them, and gave them to his disciples to distribute." Hearing the gospel account, we can acknowledge that we hear words like that every Sunday during the consecration. As Jesus gave the loaves to his disciples to distribute, so at communion time the priest gives the body and the blood of the Lord to ministers to distribute to the people.

Rationalists who insist that miracles are impossible look for some explanation for the feeding of the five thousand. Some of them want to believe that the only "miracle" was that Jesus moved the people to share with each other what they had brought along on the journey. Jesus is all in favor of sharing, to be sure, but that explanation does not fit the text or its purpose. The text says nothing about the people's sharing; rather, everything is about Jesus' sharing. He is the one who made it possible for more than five thousand people to have something to eat after they had followed him all day. As much as Jesus wants us to love one another, on that day of the feeding of the five thousand Jesus showed his love for the people as their true shepherd, just as he shows the same loving care for us in the celebration of the Eucharist.

What of the fish? The first Christians would immediately have thought of the identity of Jesus and his mission because of an acronym. The letters of the Greek word for fish, IXTHUS, are the initial letters of the words in Greek for the phrase, "Jesus Christ, God's Son, Savior." Jesus' identity is that he is the Son of God; his mission in the world is that he is the Savior. The evangelists included the fish in their account, not only because they were part of the original event, but because fish had taken on a symbolic meaning.

Remember the marriage feast at Cana? At Mass Jesus does not change water into wine; rather he changes bread and wine into his body and blood. Remember the widow of Naim? Jesus raised the widow's son to life, but only for a time on this earth. Eventually the young boy died, but the Eucharist is the food which will sustain us for life without end in heaven. Remember the fever afflicting Peter's mother-in-law? The Eucharist offers forgiveness for the sickness of sin.

I am not that lad whom I yearned to be in my youth (*wherever* I got the image). By God's grace, I am a priest who according to Catholic doctrine bears the person of Christ the priest. My favorite day of the week is Sunday when I can celebrate Mass, the fulfillment of the meaning of the loaves and the fish, with God's holy people, the assembly who are so beautiful that they look like lovely flower beds, not because of their clothing, but because of their faith. We believe the words of Jesus, "The bread that I will give is my flesh for the life of the world." We respond, "Lord, to whom shall we go? You have the words of everlasting life."

Reflection and Discussion

- St. John composed his sixth chapter in such a way that every detail was intended to make us think of the Eucharist. What are some details of daily life that make you think of the Eucharist?

- Think about people at Sunday Mass. Visualize them in your mind. How do these people today reflect the people for whom Jesus performed his great miracle of feeding the five thousand?

- Are there other episodes in the gospels, other than the Last Supper narratives, which make you think of the Eucharist?

– 1 6 –

WE NEED AUTHENTIC CATHOLICISM

…hold fast to the traditions you were taught…. (2 Thess 2:15)

When I was ordained in 1956 Catholics were not desig-
nated as liberal or conservative. We saw no need for these clas-
sifications, which essentially are political labels. We thought of
everyone in the church as being in the center, neither to the
right nor to the left in personal convictions. We told each other
that the church had never changed, that it had always remained
the same, and that throughout the whole world the Mass was
celebrated in Latin in exactly the same way. Of course none of
this was accurate, but the conviction of immutability led us to
ignore any deviations we may have witnessed or to treat them
simply as erroneous. We were taught: *Roma locuta est, causa
finita est;* that is, when Rome has spoken, the matter is settled.

In the turmoil of our era labels are inevitable, but are they
accurate? I try to listen attentively to what people are saying
these days about the liturgy and to read carefully what others are
writing. I have come to the conclusion that our labels, if these
distasteful categories are to be used at all, need updating. In
what follows please tolerate my generalities for the sake of this
discussion.

Let us begin with those who are thought of as being on the
extreme right. They want "to reform the reform." They favor a
return to Latin, and indeed to the missal of Pope Pius V (often

referred to as "the Tridentine Mass"). They tolerate no deviation from the liturgical text and reject inclusive language. They want to replace contemporary music with Gregorian Chant, to limit servers and lectors to the male sex, and to permit special ministers of holy communion under only extraordinary circumstances, if at all. They spurn communion in the hand, reject communion from the cup, and suspect that many people are going to communion while in the state of mortal sin. They prefer kneeling to standing in almost every instance. They adamantly oppose the renovation of churches and threaten to cut off all financial support to pastors who oppose their demands. They want to reverse the direction of the altar and put the tabernacle on it. Overdrawn? Yes, but only in the sense that no single person adheres to every one of these positions. At least, I do not think so.

Then there are those who are thought of as being on the *extreme* left. They advocate everything which those on the right oppose. They reject a rigid conformity to liturgical laws and prefer to improvise prayers rather than to follow established texts, even for the eucharistic prayer. They see no need for vestments and resist whatever seems to suggest a separation between clergy and laity. They want the liturgy to be adapted to cultural and local customs without recourse to any authority. They believe that whoever can preach the best homily should do so, whether that happens to be the priest or not. They favor the ordination of women and find no problem in ordaining homosexuals living with a partner. Is that enough to give you a picture?

Those on the right generally refer to themselves as conservatives. It must be said that they are actually regressive. The conservative position wishes to preserve established values and to oppose changes. To conserve means to keep something from being damaged or lost. We must not either damage or lose what has been established by the Second Vatican Council. Its liturgical principles were incorporated into a new Sacramentary and

Lectionary by Pope Paul VI. Those liturgical books have been the established norms for our celebration of the Eucharist since 1970. Later adaptations, such as the General Instruction 2000, have a firm foundation in these norms. They represent the status quo which the true conservative upholds. To return to the past is not conservative but regressive.

Those on the left generally refer to themselves as liberal. They must remember that liberalism within the structures of authority led to the reform of the previous liturgy in a way which marked real progress toward the establishment of sound principles of worship. The liberal liturgical revival which led to the Second Vatican Council traces back to the pontificate of Pope Leo XIII whose election in 1878 marked the beginning of the modern papacy. Pope Paul VI, in his *Apostolic Constitution* of April 3, 1969, insisted that the movement for reform actually began long before the pontificate of Leo XIII. He wrote: "No one should think that the revision of the Roman Missal has come out of nowhere. The progress of liturgical studies during the last four centuries has certainly prepared the way." Papal teaching consistently supported liturgical scholarship but that teaching for the most part was communicated to neither clergy nor laity. If this papal teaching had been consistently presented to Catholics, no one would have been surprised by the reforms of the Second Vatican Council. They would have said, "It's about time."

Liturgical scholars worked persistently for reform, even though by some they were considered to be on "the lunatic fringe" of the church. Their quiet patience rather than strident rancor was rewarded by the movement of the Holy Spirit within the Second Vatican Council. Liturgical scholarship was recognized by the bishops who passed the *Constitution on the Sacred Liturgy* by a vote of 2,147 in favor and only four against (history has cast her merciful veil over the names of the dissenting bishops).

What the liturgy needs at the present is authentic Catholicism. Those on the right must abandon their regressive opinions and acknowledge that the liturgy mandated by the Second Vatican Council and implemented by Pope Paul VI and post-conciliar decrees is valid, correct, and proper. It is quite unacceptable to deny the validity of the Council or the actions of the Holy See. In some instances the reform has been implemented badly, it must be admitted, but that is no reason to return to the past. Liberals on their part must recognize that, although more progress in the liturgy is needed, it is not accomplished by unauthorized changes that dismay many Catholics, antagonize a number of bishops, and move some people into regressive positions.

Very sadly the liturgy that should unite us has become a battle ground of division. Bullets of bitterness are being shot between the right and the left while most Catholics stand in the middle. These Catholics have suffered wounds, sometimes fatal ones. Can we believe that God is pleased by this battle?

The Holy Spirit is about to give us a chance to begin again. At this moment of writing there is an expectation that very soon the revised Roman Missal will be promulgated together with its General Instruction. Some complained that not enough catechesis was given in 1970; now we will have an opportunity to correct that lack. We must heed the exhortation of the *Constitution on the Sacred Liturgy*: "With zeal and patience pastors of souls must promote liturgical instruction of the faithful as well as their active participation in the liturgy both internally and externally" (19). Everyone must be prepared to accept and follow the revised liturgical books. We must give these revisions a chance to work. Their implementation will represent a grace for the American Church, and indeed for the universal church, to embark upon the reform with zeal and enlightenment and to experience the wisdom of the Second Vatican Council. That wisdom is found in the basic principles of the *Constitution on the Sacred Liturgy*, which must still guide us.

Some people protest that they have read the Constitution and find no mention of some of the changes, such as turning the altar to face the people, taking communion in the hand, or standing for holy communion. They should be informed that the Constitution gave broad principles which are carried out by means of the *General Instruction of the Roman Missal* and post-conciliar decrees. One should not expect to find everything in the Constitution, even though its principles underlie all subsequent directives.

What we do find in the Constitution is this fundamental truth which I have already cited: "Zeal for the promotion and restoration of the liturgy is rightly held to be a sign of the providential disposition of God in our time, as a movement of the Holy Spirit in his Church. It is today a distinguishing mark of the Church's life, indeed of the whole tenor of contemporary religious thought and action" (43).

The British say, "In America you drive on the right side of the road. In England we drive on the correct side of the road." To give the liturgy its due at this time, we all need to pull away from both the right and the left, to move toward the center, and to become authentic Catholics in the correct sense of that term.

Reflection and Discussion

- Can you give a description of what could rightly be called true conservatism?

- What is your understanding of tradition in human experience, perhaps in your family, and Tradition in the life of the church (lower and upper case for the word *tradition* used here intentionally)?

- What in your judgment are the most significant changes in the liturgy since the Second Vatican Council?

LITURGY:
A HOME FOR LEARNING

O magnify the Lord with me, and let us exalt his name together.
(Ps 34:3)

I return in this chapter to the indispensable element of being a Catholic: the celebration of the liturgy, which should give joy to Catholic living. It is sad these days that the word *liturgy* often suggests bitter disputes rather than joyful worship. It is a tragic waste of energy to attempt to drag people back into a pre-Vatican II era of liturgy. That energy should be used to penetrate more deeply into the restoration and renewal of the liturgy that the Council declared to be the providential disposition of God in our times. I have attempted to present in this chapter the restored liturgy as a source of learning. I am convinced that learning from the liturgy can lead to an appreciation of the liturgy itself, as well as to a deep understanding and practice of our faith.

When we speak about learning I suppose we think first of schools and teachers, of books and examinations. But environment is also a teacher. That is why parents have to be concerned about the TV shows and movies their children watch, the music they listen to, and the boys and girls they choose as their friends. The first environment in which we learn, for good or for ill, is the home, the family. Of course the family is not a school. Primarily its purpose is not learning, but loving. The good home is not a matter of the mind as much as it is a matter of the heart. Although much learning goes on in the home, such learning is not automatic. Some children pick up on it right away and others do not. Children at times need to have explained to them quite explicitly what the family stands for and what it means.

The liturgy is the family life of the church. Of course we learn outside the experience of liturgy, and that learning is very important, whether it is in the home, a Catholic school, or in religious education classes. We must not, however, neglect the liturgy as a learning experience, even though liturgy is primarily a matter of the heart rather than of the mind. Liturgy is about loving. It is not a course in theology or a catechism lesson; it is worship. The church is not a classroom; it is the house of God and our home. Granted all that, we benefit greatly from seeing that a secondary aspect of liturgy is its power to teach. In fact, the great fathers of the church knew no other source for teaching than the liturgy. Following their example, one of the models for teaching within the Rite of Christian Initiation of Adults is a form of instruction that is based on the liturgy's lectionary.

Some people pick up on the liturgy almost instinctively, but most of us need a little help to understand why we should learn from the liturgy and how to go about it. Liturgy encompasses not only the celebration of the Eucharist, but also the other six sacraments, the Liturgy of the Hours, and the liturgical year.

There are basically two reasons why we must draw teaching from the liturgy. The first is that participation in the liturgy is the primary and indispensable source from which the faithful are to derive the true Christian spirit. The second is that "the liturgy is the outstanding means by which the faithful express in their lives, and manifest to others, the mystery of Christ and the real nature of the true Church." Long before Vatican II, back in 1947, Pope Pius XII wrote in *Mediator Dei*: "In the sacred liturgy we profess the Catholic faith explicitly and openly....The entire liturgy has the Catholic faith for its content." Later, in sending a message to the Assisi Congress, the same pope wrote: "It would be difficult to find a truth of the Christian faith which is not somehow expressed in the liturgy, whether it is the readings from the Old and the New Testament in the Mass and the Divine Office, or the riches which mind and heart discover in the psalms." And from time immemorial the church has adhered to the axiom *lex orandi, lex credendi*—literally, "the law of praying is the law of believing." The meaning is that the way in which we pray expresses what we believe. It is not surprising that some people objected to the liturgical reforms of the Second Vatican Council since, although a change in liturgy does not alter our doctrine, it does affect our understanding of it. Liturgy not only contains doctrine but gives it a flavor from the manner in which the liturgy is celebrated. Two cooks might prepare the same menu, but one might turn out a meal which is more nutritious and more flavorful than did the other.

There are three basic questions we ought to ask about every liturgical experience: (1) What does it say about God? (2) What does it say about the community which is the church? (3) What does it say about the Eucharist?

The reasons for these three questions are (1) that all liturgy is worship of God, and therefore acknowledges something about him; (2) that liturgy is never private or individual, but rather reflects the truth that it has pleased God to save us and make us holy, not merely as individuals without any mutual bonds but by forming us into a single people, the church; and (3) that the eucharistic celebration is the summit toward which all the activity of the church is directed, as well as the source from which all her power flows.

The three basic questions, then, concerning every liturgical experience are: (1) What does it say about God? (2) What does it say about the community? (3) What does it say about the Eucharist? These questions can be expanded to include specifics, such as: What does the liturgy teach about prayer, the purpose of life, relations with others, duties to work for justice and peace?

The liturgy is our teacher in four principal ways: (1) the setting or atmosphere of liturgical celebration, (2) the content of its prayers, especially the eucharistic prayers, (3) the re-presentation of the events of the liturgical year, and (4) the liturgy's use of sacred scripture. Even though the Eucharist is not the only form of liturgy, my examples, which I trust will stimulate thinking about the teaching value of the liturgy, will be taken from the Sunday celebration of the Mass.

First, think about the setting or atmosphere of liturgical celebration. Reflect on the fact that there is a lot of room in church for a large crowd. It is not like going to the doctor and being put in one of those little cubbyhole offices. Seeing the doctor is private, between just two people. Religion is not just between me and God; it necessarily involves people. These people form the body of Christ, the mystical body of Christ, the church. During the Mass we should be conscious of people beside us and those around the altar. We readily notice the priest. He is taking the place of the bishop and is the sign of the unity of the church as he acts "in the person of Christ." If the liturgy is celebrated correctly, the priest does not act virtually alone, as he used to do in the Tridentine Mass. The liturgy which we inherited from Pope Pius V in 1570 reflected a certain ecclesiology, our way of looking at the church. When I was first ordained, the priest did everything at Mass because the priest did everything in the life of the church. If the priest did not direct some project, it was usually not considered to be Catholic. That was the ecclesiology which shaped the liturgy. The liturgy given to us by Pope Paul VI in 1970 reflects the ecclesiology of the Second Vatican Council. Now at Mass we should see people involved in different functions: the cantor, the readers, the servers, the eucharistic ministers—the more the better to suggest the variety of the church as the body of Christ and the multiple ministries which are provided for God's people. The liturgical ministers are properly robed in albs, the white garment which is the sign of baptism. Through baptism we have been incorporated into the priestly people of God. All liturgy, but in particular the setting, should lead us to the truth, the ecclesiology, simply but profoundly expressed by the Second Vatican Council: "It has pleased God to save us and to make us holy, not merely as individuals without any mutual bonds, but by forming us into a single people, a people who worship him in truth and who serve him in holiness."

The liturgical setting reflects the theology of the incarnation. All creation is sacred because it has come from the holy hand of God, but when the eternal Son of God "did not spurn the Virgin's womb," as we say in the *Te Deum,* he gave a special dignity and value to all things material and manifested that God is present and active in and through his creation. The liturgy, drawing on this truth, reminds us that we do not live in two worlds—one religious and one secular. We live in God's world. That is why in the celebration of liturgy we use elements from life on this planet: music, paintings, statues, candles, vestments, incense, decorations, water, oil, bread, wine, and so forth. That is also why the liturgy is external as well as internal, and why it involves hearts and hands and voices. The liturgy is worship by the whole person, in our material as well as our spiritual aspects. Some forms of spirituality would have us believe that true piety consists only in divorcing ourselves from people and separating ourselves from our surroundings. Catholic liturgy teaches a different lesson, the profoundly beautiful truth of the presence and action of God in the people and the objects of his creation.

Next we think about the prayers. The great richness of the liturgical prayers links us with our tradition and reaches back through the centuries beyond the schools of spirituality and theology that reflected an understanding of the church which was common just prior to the renewal of the Second Vatican

Council. People of my generation knew the answer to the question, "Why did God make me?" As children we quickly responded, "God made me to know him, to love him, and to serve him in this world, in order to be happy with him in the next." That is a good answer, especially considering its brevity. It instructed a very large number of Catholics in the United States from the year 1885 when Bishop John Lancaster Spalding of Peoria, Illinois and Father Joseph de Concilio of Newark, New Jersey composed the *Baltimore Catechism*. It does lack, however, the richness of a biblical and traditional approach which is found in liturgical prayer. As a consequence it is highly individualistic and more philosophical than theological, in accord with the status of scholarship at the time it was originally written. Reflect, in contrast, on the words of one of the Sunday Prefaces that are a prayer of praise to God the Father, but that offer instruction to us: "You chose to create men and women in your own image, setting them over the whole world in all its wonder. You made them the stewards of creation, to praise you day by day for the marvels of your wisdom and power." Add to this the beauty of God's plan for us as expressed in another Preface that is drawn from the First Epistle of St. Peter: "Through his cross and resurrection [Christ] freed us from sin and death and called us to the glory that has made us a chosen race, a royal priesthood, a holy nation, a people set apart. Everywhere we proclaim your mighty works for you have called us out of darkness into your own wonderful light."

Liturgical prayers are expressed in accord with the way God has revealed himself to us in the Christian era so that our prayers of petition, as a norm, are addressed to the Father through the Son in the Holy Spirit, and our prayers of praise and thanks are always offered to the Father in the manner expressed in the great doxology: "Through him [Christ], with him, in him, in the unity of the Holy Spirit all glory and honor is yours, almighty Father, forever and ever." The form of these prayers and other words in the liturgy manifest that God is our Father, we are his children in Christ, united by the love of the Holy Spirit. We not only pray as Jesus taught us by calling upon God as Father but we ourselves are addressed as brothers and sisters to indicate the relationship which we have with each other.

The prayers, and not only the scriptures, manifest the meaning of the feast days which we celebrate. In pondering the meaning of Christmas, for example, we can think about this Preface for the Solemnity of the Nativity: "Today you fill our hearts with joy as we recognize in Christ the revelation of your love. No eye can see his glory as our God, yet now he is seen as one like us. Christ is your Son before all ages, yet now he is born in time. He has come to lift up all things to himself, to restore unity to creation, and to lead all mankind from exile into your heavenly kingdom."

The prayers of the liturgy will always give us a perfect balance. It is vital that we see God as transcendent, far above us, not limited by our poor, tiny brains. On the other hand we must realize that in Christ God has become immanent, close to us, like us in all things but sin. Within every eucharistic prayer we first cry out: "Holy, holy, holy Lord, God of power and might. Heaven and earth are full of your glory." These words are drawn from the vision which Isaiah had of the magnificence of God. The triple "holy" suggests the superlative degree, and proclaims that God is transcendent, far beyond what we can experience or imagine. To the triple holy we quickly add: "Blessed is he who comes in the name of the Lord." These words, from Psalm 118, were applied to Jesus on Passion [Palm] Sunday when he concluded his journey to Jerusalem where he was to undergo his passion and death, and are the most striking manifestation of his humanity and the most compelling sign of God's immanence: the Son of God became human like us in all things but sin, subject to suffering and even to death. The liturgy is always the safe guide for a balanced theology as well as a sound piety.

The liturgy goes to the heart of the Christian paschal mystery. During the eucharistic prayer the priest proclaims that the real presence of Christ is the sacrament of the mystery of faith. That mystery is the truth that "Christ has died; Christ is risen; Christ will come again." The meaning of this truth we express by proclaiming to Christ himself: "Dying you destroyed our death; rising you restored our life." We elaborate on the truth when to Christ we say: "Lord, by your cross and resurrection, you have set us free. You are the Savior of the world." We acknowledge that the eucharistic celebration is a sacramental sharing in the paschal mystery when we declare, "When we eat this bread and drink this cup, we proclaim your death, Lord Jesus, until you come in glory."

The liturgy also teaches us by the annual reliving of the events of the liturgical year. These events help us to see that theology is not an abstraction, and that God reveals himself to us through concrete events of salvation history. The liturgy does not merely state that God is good and loving; rather, the liturgy helps us to recognize that "God so loved the world that he gave his only Son, that whoever believes in him may not die but may have eternal life." In the liturgy we relive that event from the incarnation through the death and resurrection of Jesus to the sending of the Holy Spirit at Pentecost. The liturgy is a story that each year unfolds the truth which we proclaim to God in the fourth eucharistic prayer: "Father, all your actions show your wisdom and love." Through participating in this story—the mystery of God that is ever made present and active for us within the liturgy by the power of the Holy Spirit—we draw closer to the person of Christ who is the truth of the Father, the way to the Father, and the life of the Father.

A profound way in which the liturgy teaches us is by the manner in which it uses the Bible. The Bible is not a single book; it is a library of many books. It was composed, as we now have it, over a period of perhaps 1200 years. Many human authors, living in different eras and having varied backgrounds and concerns, are responsible for the Bible under the guidance of the Holy Spirit. The Bible is the work of human beings, and yet it truly is the Word of God. The unifying principle of this library is that ultimately there is but one divine author, the Holy Spirit. That is why the liturgy on Sundays of Ordinary Time begins its scriptural selections with a reading from the Old Testament, which may have been composed seven hundred years before the birth of Christ and links that reading with a gospel pericope that was composed approximately seventy years after the birth of Christ.

The liturgy claims the Bible as its own, not only because portions of it were composed to be read within the assembly of the faithful, but because God's communication through the scriptures is not to individuals but to a community, first to Israel and then to the church. Liturgically the Bible is proclaimed within the community to manifest its ecclesial character. It is not an object of private interpretation but the living voice of Christ in his church since "it is Christ himself who speaks when the holy scriptures are read in the church."

We can deepen our understanding of our faith through four principal aspects of the liturgy: the setting, the prayers, the liturgical year, and the way the liturgy uses the Bible. Contained within these four realities are beautiful and sound answers to three fundamental questions: What does the liturgy say about God? What does the liturgy say about the church? What does the liturgy say about the Eucharist?

The *Constitution on the Sacred Liturgy* presents the basic principle regarding the teaching power of the liturgy: "Although the sacred liturgy is above all things the worship of the divine Majesty, it likewise contains abundant instruction for the faithful" (33). Not only the Bible, but the entire liturgy "is useful for teaching, reproof, correction, and training in righteousness" (see 2 Tim 3:16). Learning from the liturgy leads us, I believe, to value the liturgy itself. Ultimately the liturgy is our best teacher because it is the family life of God's children.

Reflection and Discussion

- What impact does hearing the scriptures and the homily at Mass have on you?

- How can you enter more fully into the celebration of the Mass?

- Think about the experience of living the liturgical year that extends from Advent to the Solemnity of Christ the King. What are you especially conscious of from this experience?

LITURGY NEEDS A SOUL

New wine must he put into fresh wineskins. (Luke 5:38)

A parish has done everything that is required by the restored liturgy. The people sing well in response to the direction of a trained cantor and offer the prayers with some enthusiasm. Lectors proclaim the readings clearly and intelligently. Special ministers of the Eucharist offer the body and blood of the Lord respectfully, and people avail themselves of the privilege of receiving from the cup. The priest-presider is friendly yet reverent and gives an interesting seven-minute homily which is drawn appropriately from the liturgy of the day and is pertinent to life. But something seems missing. All the externals are correct, but the soul—an invisible, life-giving, and unifying force—is not there.

The theology of that community is not in accord with the theology of the liturgy. The fault does not lie with anyone in the parish. For a very long time most Catholics have been schooled in a theology and piety that were not derived from liturgical sources, and were therefore not supportive of liturgical celebration. When Pope Paul VI promulgated the restored missal in accord with the directives of the Second Vatican Council, it seemed that proper implementation would accomplish the goals which the fathers of the council had in mind. Some observed that the restoration was not accepted by some Catholics because the new rites were not sufficiently explained to them. The truth is that a complete explanation was impossible without a return to a more traditional theology, which is drawn from the Bible and the writings of the early fathers of the church. This theology is called scriptural and patristic. We should have heeded the warning of Jesus: "New wine must be put into fresh wineskins."

The *Constitution on the Sacred Liturgy* (11) placed a heavy burden on bishops and priests. It declared that "pastors of souls must realize that, when the liturgy is celebrated, more is required than the mere observance of the laws governing valid and licit celebration. It is their duty also to assure that the faithful take part knowingly, actively, and fruitfully." This was a difficult assignment because pastors of souls had many obstacles to overcome in implementing three seemingly simple adverbs regarding participation in the liturgy: knowingly, actively, and fruitfully.

People in general understood very little about liturgy. They came to it as to a private prayer and generally preferred novenas and devotions over the liturgy. It did not seem to them, as the Council taught, that "every liturgical celebration, because it is an action of Christ the priest and of his body, the Church, is a sacred action surpassing all others, and that no other action of the Church can match its claim to efficacy nor equal the degree of it" (*Constitution on the Sacred Liturgy*, 7).

Many Catholics had not been instructed in the doctrines that the liturgy proclaims and upon which it is founded. In response to the question, "Why did God make me?" many Catholics can still recite the formula: "God made me to know him, to love him, and to serve him in this world so that I might be happy with him in the next." The liturgy requires that this formula be expanded through the trinitarian, incarnational, and ecclesial aspects of our Catholic faith to form a new wineskin for the restored liturgy. Liturgical theology begins with the truth that God is Father, Son, and Spirit. It invites us to see that we have been drawn into this family life of God. We acknowledge in the third eucharistic prayer: "Father, all life, all holiness comes from you through your Son, our Lord Jesus Christ by the working of the Holy Spirit." We believe that the Son in becoming human has become our priest, our mediator with the Father, our intercessor.

Liturgically we stand in the person of Christ, our priest, united as part of his body, the church, by the Holy Spirit to worship God the Father. This trinitarian orientation is expressed mightily in the doxology of the eucharistic prayer: "Through him, with him, in him, in the unity of the Holy Spirit, all glory and honor is yours, almighty Father, forever and ever." Prayers of petition also are trinitarian since we address them to the Father "through our Lord, Jesus Christ, your Son, who lives and reigns with you and the Holy Spirit, one God, forever and ever." We address Jesus as our intercessor with the Father as we exclaim: "Lord, have mercy."

In scriptural and patristic theology, to know God means to acknowledge him as Father. To love God is to respond to him as his devoted children. To serve God is to work lovingly for him as part of his family. To be happy is to begin, even while on this earth, to share in our heavenly inheritance through an active, devout life in the church. Liturgy insists that God did more than make us. He begot us as his beloved sons and daughters. He is much more than our creator; he is our Father. "He destined us for adoption as his children through Jesus Christ,...to the praise of his glorious grace..." (Eph 1:5). We do not serve God in order to win some favor as did the older boy in the parable of the prodigal son. We work for God because we are his family members. We know that God gives us all good things without our merit and that heaven is ours as an inheritance, not a reward. We have in fact been "marked with the seal of the promised Holy Spirit,...the pledge of our inheritance" (Eph 1:13–14). We do not stand before God in isolation from one another. We are God's family, brothers and sisters of one another.

The purity of this trinitarian doctrine has been tainted by what theologians call "Christo-monism," a form of piety that correctly sees Christ as God but quite erroneously fails to acknowledge his place in the Trinity to the detriment of the doctrine of God as Father. It has also obscured the image of Jesus, the incarnate God, as our intercessor, our priest. This error, which is the result of extremism in protesting the divinity of Christ, developed a long time ago within Catholicism in reaction to the christological heresies. Now it has become the religion of TV evangelists and the like. Catholic doctrine is that Jesus is God, that he is one divine person, and that his personhood is a filial relationship to God the Father.

Although Christo-monism acknowledges that Jesus is Lord, it fails in practice to see him as Son. Christo-monism looks upon Christ in the holy Eucharist as the object of our adoration rather than as our priest and victim, our intercessor, who invites us to join him in offering the holy sacrifice to the honor and glory of his Father. Christ explained to his disciples that he is the way to the Father, he is the truth of the Father, he is the life of the Father. He directs us to the Father so that we may have the disposition of love and devotion which is his personhood in the Trinity. There are not three persons in God so that we may have a choice of which person appeals to us. God is, as the theologians say, subsistent relationships. The Father's plan is that we share the relationship which is Son through the Spirit, the personified love between Father and Son. All of this illustrates that it was, and is, a demanding task to get people to participate "knowingly."

Active participation was for many people a strange innovation at Mass since they were used to Mass in Latin. To most Catholics piety meant a quiet, if not silent, reserved form of prayer, a raising of the mind and heart to God, alone with the Lord. The manner in which Mass was said provided a reverent atmosphere for their individual expressions of piety, and they felt a sense of awe and mystery in the arcane rites which unfolded beyond their sight. Now some Catholics protest that these elements are not evident in the restored liturgy. Many in practice have resisted a profound principle of the Council: "In the restoration and promotion of the sacred liturgy, the full and active participation by all the people is the aim to be considered above all else, for it is the primary and indispensable source of the true Christian spirit" (*Constitution on the Sacred Liturgy,* 14). A reversal of thinking is necessary to recognize that a deep reverence is found in acts of worship which include all aspects of our humanity, and a profound sense of awe results from the clearer understanding that the restored rites provide. We need an appreciation of the doctrine of the incarnation which teaches us that human nature, already holy as coming from the creative hand of God, was given a special sacredness by the conception and birth of the Son of God. That is why the liturgy relies on the truth that our minds and hearts are fully raised to God in prayer through the use of all aspects of our humanity—our actions as well as our minds and our voices as well as our hearts. Liturgy follows the injunction of sacred scripture: "...with gratitude in your hearts sing psalms, hymns, and spiritual songs to God" (Col 3:16; see also Eph 5:19). All of this illustrates that it has been difficult, and still is, to get people to participate "actively."

To participate fruitfully, as the liturgy intends, requires a generous, outgoing, and unselfish spirit. The primary purpose of liturgy is to offer worship to God in union with the universal church, and the local church in particular. The complaint, "I don't get anything out of Mass," may be occasioned by poorly celebrated liturgy, but often it reflects the narcissistic individualism of our society with its demand for personal fulfillment. Even those forms of spirituality which center almost exclusively on personal growth unwittingly militate against the liturgical spirit which wishes to draw us out of ourselves, away from self-preoccupation, to embrace God the Father and all his children in our love and prayerful concern.

A typically American expression of religion declares that "Jesus is my personal Lord and Savior." That declaration sullies the wineskins with individualism. We may think that this approach to religion has not affected us as Catholics but individualism has become so pervasive in American society that it has influenced every aspect of our lives. That is why the Supreme Court could invent the notion of "right to privacy" and why a California senator, now deceased, could dogmatically declare that the most fundamental right of all Americans is the right to choose. It is also why some Catholics find it annoying to have to relate to other people during the liturgy. In contrast to individualism in religion, the liturgical image of the church is that of a family. Liturgical prayers use family words. They speak of God as Father, as Son, and as the Spirit of family love. They refer to us as brothers and sisters of one another in Christ and ask the Father to hear the prayers of the family which stands before him. They speak of eternal life as our inheritance, the gift which children receive from their parents, which we will share with all the saints, our brothers and sisters in heaven, which is our home. The church is more than a society to which we belong in order to derive spiritual support and to benefit by an eternal life insurance policy. The church is the family of God on this earth. We come together for liturgy not as isolated individuals but as children of one Father. A paramount doctrine of the Second Vatican Council, actually its central idea, is this statement which I must repeat: "It has pleased God to save us and to make us holy, not merely as individuals without any mutual bonds, but by forming us into a single people, a people who worship him in truth and who serve him in holiness" (*Dogmatic Constitution on the Church*, 9). It has been, and remains, a challenge to get people to participate "fruitfully."

Can it be done? Can we allow the rich wine of the liturgy to be a spirit that fills a new wineskin of liturgical theology and gives life to all of our worship? First, we must not turn away from the task either because of an inclination to surrender to weariness and frustration, or because of a temptation to think that liturgical renewal is not worthwhile or even correct. We must not cling to the trappings of the past or indulge a nostalgia for an era which actually was far from ideal. Equally we should not accept the notion that abuses and aberrations are an expression of the "spirit" of the liturgy. Above all we must allow well prepared and fully celebrated liturgy to speak to us, to teach us, and to form us. We need docility which includes an eagerness to learn from the liturgy itself, without imposing upon it preconceived ideas, because liturgy is an authentic expression of our faith. As the Council began its declaration of liturgical principles it stated: "The liturgy is the outstanding means by which the faithful can express in their lives and manifest to others the mystery of Christ and the real nature of the true Church" (*Constitution on the Sacred Liturgy*, 2).

We must not let the teachings of the Council die. In particular, we must continue all our efforts to insure that "the faithful take part in the liturgy knowingly, actively, and fruitfully." For our motivation and inspiration we continually return to this profound truth from the *Constitution on the Sacred Liturgy* (43): "Zeal for the promotion and restoration of the liturgy is rightly held to be a sign of the providential disposition of God in our times, as a movement of the Holy Spirit in his Church. It is today a distinguishing mark of the Church's life."

Reflection and Discussion

● What exactly did Jesus mean when he said that new wine must be put into fresh wineskins? Are there examples in the gospel of what he meant?

- Think about these three adverbs: knowingly, actively, fruitfully. Are they fulfilled for you by your manner of participating in the Mass?

- How can you contribute to the "soul" of the liturgy in your parish?

THREE WAYS
TO BE A CATHOLIC

"Be perfect, therefore, as your heavenly Father is perfect."
(Matt 5:48)

I began this simple book on being Catholic by referring to Father Leonard Feeney's book, *Fish on Friday,* and I explained why I chose the title *Mass on Sunday.* Some of my thinking was based on the teaching of the Second Vatican Council that "the liturgy is the summit toward which the activity of the Church is directed, as well as the fountain from which all her power flows" (*Constitution on the Sacred Liturgy*, 10). The Council also gave strong endorsement to Sunday as "our original feast day" and as the pre-eminent day for the celebration of the Eucharist. Hence my title, *Mass on Sunday.* Actually it is impossible to sum up the meaning of being a Catholic in the succinct title of a book.

The Second Vatican Council throughout its sixteen documents, but especially in its *Dogmatic Constitution on the Church,* emphasized that Catholics are not to be passive members of the church as if the church were merely an institution to which they belonged. The Council relied on the New Testament teaching of the church as the body of Christ to explain that together we all form the church, each of us with our own calling from God to fill out the body of Christ. The *Constitution on the Sacred Liturgy* (2) insisted on full, active, conscious participation in the liturgy because the liturgy is "the outstanding means by which Catholics may express in their lives and manifest to others the mystery of Christ and the real nature of the true Church." Most Catholics seem to think that Vatican II was primarily about the liturgy, but actually its topic was the church. The liturgy had to change in order to express a renewed and deeper understanding of the church, which was drawn from the teachings of scripture and the fathers of the church. Even now these many years after the conclusion of the Council we are still struggling to be the church of Vatican II.

One alternative to the church of Vatican II is the church of compromise. The church of compromise provides a way of spending part of Sunday with God but not of dedicating one's entire life to God. Catholics in this expression of the church consider themselves to be good people, and they probably are, but their goals, aspirations, and values are no different from those of the secular, materialistic society in which we live. Some of them expect the church to provide a kind of eternal life insurance, but they usually want no involvement in social issues and think that the church should stick to saving souls. The extent of their rejection of the errors of their contemporaries is that they generally feel that abortion is not a good thing. For the most part they approve of the death penalty. They tend to agree that we should shut all doors to immigrants and force young mothers on welfare to leave their children and to take jobs. Their inclination is to favor spending billions on weapons while cutting funds for public housing. A number of them are confounded by the gospel predilection for the poor and infuriated by the bishops' pronouncements regarding economic and social issues. In these matters they say of the church, *"Mater, sí; magistra, no"* (mother, yes; teacher, no). While leaning toward contempt for the homeless, they forget that their ability, their intelligence, their industry, and their opportunities are gifts from God, and that some people, for whatever reasons, are not as gifted as they. The renewed liturgy, which is the expression that we are God's people, usually finds little favor with them. The sad fact is that we may belong completely or in part to the church of compromise.

The church of compromise, despite my bleak description, is not entirely bad. After all, compromise involves giving up some principles while retaining others. Religious compromise stands somewhere between total rejection of Catholicism and embracing the church of comfort. People in the church of comfort are very good Catholics. They are faithful to Sunday Mass, respond to the almost monthly appeals to fund worthy causes, and they volunteer to be lectors, eucharistic ministers, ushers, religious education teachers, and ministers to the youth and the elderly. They may attend Mass daily or at least more often than just on Sunday, show up for penance services, and are dedicated to one or more forms of personal devotions, such as the rosary. Some pray at least part of the Liturgy of the Hours daily. They are the people the pastor can depend on to visit the sick, take the elderly to the doctor, do the shopping for shut-ins, and be willing to help in almost any parish function. To be a Catholic in the church of comfort is a very satisfying, fulfilling way to live.

People in the church of comfort are indeed very good Catholics. In fact, all of their admirable qualities are intensified in the church of commitment. What else then can be required of Catholics in the church of commitment without asking them to become Trappist monks or cloistered nuns? Obvious examples of people in the church of commitment are Pope John Paul II, Mother Teresa of Calcutta, and Archbishop Oscar Romero, but they seem too extraordinary to be realistic models. Observant people can name some fellow parishioners as examples of commitment—perhaps a single person who heroically cares for aging parents and anyone else who needs her; maybe an exemplary married couple who are unusually dedicated parents and yet find time to help even those outside their family, or a deeply caring pastor, bishop, or religious sister—all generally unheralded.

Most important for our era is the fact the people in the church of commitment have read the signs of the times together with Pope John XXIII. They embrace the Vatican Council as the supreme and definitive teaching of the church, which is God's will for our era. They are convinced that "zeal for the promotion and restoration of the liturgy is rightly held to be a sign of the providential dispositions of God in our time, as a movement of the Holy Spirit in his Church." They worship in accord with the declaration that "in the restoration and promotion of the sacred liturgy the aim to be considered before all else is the full and active participation by all the faithful, for it is the primary and indispensable source from which the faithful are to derive the true Christian spirit" (see the *Constitution on the Sacred Liturgy,* 43 and 14).

The true Christian spirit which is taught and nourished by the liturgy leads to a life of commitment to the ideals of scripture and the other teachings of the church, especially those which involve charity and social justice. The liturgical pioneers of the twentieth century, led by the Benedictine Dom Virgil Michel, were convinced that a renewed liturgy would motivate people to implement the ideals of Christ's kingdom—in particular the virtues of justice, love, and peace. They intuitively made the step from authentic worship to responsible action. For most of us a conscious and deliberate decision is necessary before we allow the grace of the liturgy to imbue us with the true Christian spirit.

This spirit helps Catholics to embrace what Pope John Paul II has called the culture of life in opposition to the culture of death. They understand that Cardinal Bernardin's analogy of the seamless garment symbolizes that Catholics must have a consistent pro-life ethic which recognizes that every human person is made in the image and likeness of God and redeemed by the precious blood of Jesus Christ, that rights do not depend on whether one is in or out of the womb or on the north or south side of the border, and that dignity does not depend on whether one is acceptable and valued in our individualistic, narcissistic, and materialistic society. They recognize that any form of ethnic or racial bigotry is a contradiction of what it means to be a Catholic. They live in accord with the opening statement of Vatican II's *Constitution on the Church in the Modern World:* "The joy and hope, the sorrows and the anxieties of the people of this age, especially those who are poor or in any way afflicted, are the joy and hope, the sorrows and anxieties of the followers of Christ. Indeed nothing genuinely human fails to raise an echo in their hearts, for theirs is a community of people united in Christ and led by the Holy Spirit."

Catholics in the church of commitment are not dismayed that the church favors welfare even though it needs reform, and advocates affirmative action even though it is open to abuse. These Catholics are not scandalized that their diocese has a ministry for gay and lesbian Catholics and is seeking ways to help divorced and remarried Catholics to participate fully in the life of the church. In the church of commitment the norm is the example of Jesus who welcomed sinners and ate with them, who refused to stone the woman caught in the act of adultery, who in allowing his apostles to violate the Sabbath when they were hungry showed that charity is above every human law. These Catholics remember that Jesus lived as an alien in Egypt, that he was so poor he had no place to lay his head, that he did not hesitate to associate with sinners, that he was condemned as a criminal, and spent his last moments hanging on a cross between two thieves.

Catholics in the church of commitment believe that Jesus truly lives in people, and they act in accord with the truth that whatever they do to even the least of his brothers and sisters they do to him. They know that belief in the presence of Christ in the Eucharist is incomplete without faith in the presence of Christ in people. They do not ask of those in need, "Are you worthy or unworthy, are you white or black, are you legal or illegal, are you born or unborn?" They only ask, "Are you a human being?"

Christ becomes the norm for their views and their actions, both because they see Christ in others and because they realize that Christ wants to act in and through them. They understand what St. Augustine meant when he said that the church is Christ loving Christ. Liturgy in the church of commitment is not an individualistic act of personal devotion. It is the celebration by God's people of "the wonderful works of God in the history of salvation, that is, the mystery of Christ, which is always present and active among us, especially in the actions of the sacred liturgy." They recognize that Vatican II gave us a form of liturgy we were not used to because it restored an image of the church we had lost.

Catholics in the Church of Commitment respond to the commission by the priest, or deacon, at the end of Mass, "Go in peace to love and serve the Lord." They see this not as a dismissal but as a commission. They know that it is in loving and serving their brothers and sisters that they are loving and serving the Lord. They experience peace which comes from rising above the self-centered ambition of a narcissistic approach to life. They have come to realize not only that the way we pray expresses what we believe *(lex orandi, lex credendi),* but that the way we pray must influence the way in which we live *(lex orandi, lex vivendi).*

We may be drawn to belong to a church of compromise; that is a strong temptation in our society. We may be happy to be part of a church of comfort; that is quite satisfying. We may decide to strive to be the church of commitment; that is a big step. In fact, we may at different times and under varied circumstances belong more to one church than to the others. The church of comfort and the church of commitment overlap in many ways. Only great saints are completely in the church of commitment, and then only after a long struggle to embrace the grace of God. I am embarrassed to teach and preach the church of commitment. I must confess that in at least a few ways I am in the church of compromise, although I am for the most part in the church of comfort. I know that I must continue to work toward becoming more identified with the church of commitment. I feel awkward about this, like a person who is trying to stand in three places at the same time, but I am not discouraged since I accept the challenge to grow as a Catholic and I understand that I cannot wait until I am perfect before preaching and teaching the truth.

It is not easy to change to the church of Vatican II which involves full, active participation in the restored liturgy. The price may be giving up some old, and perhaps cherished, notions of what the church and the Mass should be. The process will likely involve growing pains. But the indispensable source of the true Christian spirit, the spirit of the church of commitment, is full, active participation in the sacred liturgy. The more we try to enter into the liturgy, the more complete we become as Catholics, and the more complete we are as Catholics, the closer we come to full participation.

There remain these three: compromise, comfort, and commitment. And the greatest of these is commitment.

Reflection and Discussion

- Can you think of more characteristics of the church of compromise?

- Can you think of more characteristics of the church of comfort?

- Is it asking too much to move into the church of commitment?

– 2 0 –

HOPE INVITES US
TO A LIFE OF JOY

Rejoice in the Lord always.... (Phil 4:4)

A couple may get progressively nervous as their wedding draws near, but knowing that the big event is approaching gives zest to ordinary days. Students about to finish school must make sure they pass their exams, but thinking about graduation lightens the burden of academic work. Ballplayers get nervous as the time for an important game draws near, but they are eager for the day to come. Looking forward to a happy event is one of the joys of living. We, as Catholics, whether we are in the church of compromise or comfort or commitment, are a people who live in the present with an eye on the future. The church in the liturgy urges us to put on a happy face and to turn our focus toward the bright dawn, the light of Christ, who came into our world to dispel the dark night of sadness.

It is sad, not joyful, when people are deprived of the truth of Christ. To bring Christ to such people, Vincent Donovan, the Holy Ghost Father to whom I referred in the first chapter, spent seventeen years as a missionary in Tanzania. He worked mostly with the Masai people of East Africa who are, for the most part, illiterate. In their simple spoken language they have no future tense. They live pretty much only in the present, getting up each day to eat, drink, do their chores, and then retire for the night, only to carry out much the same routine the next day. Because they have no future tense, they have no hope.

When he tried to evangelize the Masai, Father Donovan discovered that he had not realized how vital to the Christian message is the concept of the future. He concluded, "I think you could say that one of the purposes and goals of evangelizing the Masai is to put a future tense in their language."

The Mass, especially during the rite of holy communion, emphasizes the future tense. It calls us not only to look forward to the second coming of our Savior but to do so with joy. After the Our Father we pray: "Deliver us, Lord, from every evil and grant us peace in our day. In your mercy keep us free from sin and protect us from all anxiety [good word] as we wait in joyful hope [that is the idea] for the coming of our Savior, Jesus Christ."

Some religious people think of the Second Coming as a time of dread. They are caricatured by the extremists we see now and then, dressed in long robes, who hold up signs saying, "Repent! The End is Near! Doom! Destruction!" They believe that the end of the world means annihilation. The truth is that the end of the world means completion. Think of it this way: the church you go to on Sunday for Mass was at one time nothing more than a plan, a blueprint, a hope of people and their pastor. Funds were raised, contractors and builders were hired, and work was begun. Then one day the building was completed. It was at an end. It was finished. That did not mean destruction, but just the opposite. Money and effort had been put into constructing a suitable place for worship, the church. Its completion meant that it was ready for use. It is in that sense that the world as we know it will come to an end, a completion.

The Second Vatican Council gives us the official Catholic teaching in these words: "We do not know the time for the consummation of the earth and of humanity. Nor do we know how all things will be transformed. As deformed by sin, the shape of this world will pass away, but we are taught that God is preparing a new dwelling place and a new earth where justice will abide, and whose blessedness will answer and surpass all the longings for peace which spring up in the human heart." This teaching of the church reflects the New Testament epistle of St. Peter which states: "…we wait for new heavens and a new earth, where righteousness is at home" (2 Pet 3:13).

The difference between the religious extremists and the Catholic Church is the view of God. Extremists tend to think of God as a wrathful and vengeful deity whom we must fear. Catholics see God as a faithful and loving Father who wishes the best for his children and who asks only for love in return. Extremists seem to think God is someone who will punish evil by wiping out the earth and the human race. Catholics see God as the Lord who corrects evil through the triumph of justice and peace. Finally, extremists fear that God is *de*structive. Catholics believe that God is *con*structive.

Some people pray that they may be protected from the wrath of the Lord when he comes at the end of time. In every Mass we express our joyful hope for the coming of our Savior. We may have problems now, but we know that better, not worse, times are yet to come. In fact, the best is still in the future. Our faith in the future is based on the past. As we journey through life we should constantly be looking back over our shoulder to see what God has already done, especially in the sending of his Son into the world. "For God so loved the world that he gave his only Son, so that everyone who believes in him may not perish but may have eternal life" (John 3:16). Jesus was born to die on the cross for the salvation of the whole world. God will not be frustrated. He will not waste the redeeming work of his Son. At the end of the time allotted to this world in its present condition, he will not conclude that it was all a mistake to be erased from his memory. No, he will make sure that the work of his Son which was begun on this earth will be brought to completion.

St. Paul wrote to the Philippians words which we hear as addressed to ourselves: "I am confident of this, that the one who began a good work among you will bring it to completion by the day of Jesus Christ" (Phil 1:6). We can be confident that with God's grace we will, so to speak, pass our final exam. To put it another way, we will win the great game of life. Best of all, we will be with Christ in a union of undying love.

The future tense is an essential part of our religious language. Let the extremists make their signs of "Doom!" and "Destruction!" We believe in a happy future because we look to the signs which God has made: that of an infant lying in a crib and that of a God-man dying on a cross. With these signs to lead us, we journey through life in light of the truth that hope invites us to a life of joy.

Reflection and Discussion

- Blessed Columba Marmion, a Benedictine abbot, said that joy is the echo of God's life within us. Can you expand on what that means?

- St. Paul wrote, "Rejoice always" (see Phil 4:4). Is it really possible to rejoice always, even when a spouse or a parent or a child dies?

- How can you contribute to a life of joy among those with whom you live or associate?